THE GOOD FORTUNE HANDBOOK

THE GOOD FORTUNE HANDBOOK

DEVELOPING A STOIC OUTLOOK DAY BY DAY

MATTHEW J. VAN NATTA

ImStoic Publications

Portland, Oregon, USA

The Good Fortune Handbook by Matthew J. Van Natta is licensed under a Creative Commons Attribution-ShareAlike 4.0 International License, except where otherwise noted.

Contents

	The Good Fortune Handbook	vii
1.	What is Stoicism?	1
2.	A Podcast's Introduction	3
	Good Fortune: Episode One	
3.	A Stoic Start to the Day	9
	Good Fortune: Episode Two	
4.	A Stoic End to the Day	17
	Good Fortune: Episode Five	
5.	Attention is Fundamental	23
	Good Fortune: Episode Three	
6.	What We Control	29
	Good Fortune: Episode Four	
7.	Handling Distressing News	35
	Good Fortune: Episode Six	
8.	Stoicism and the Blues	41
9.	When People Are Obstacles	43
	Good Fortune: Episode Seven	
10.	How Stoics Treat Jerks	51
11.	Nine Ways to Stop Being Upset by Others	55
12.	Fighting Non-Stoic Thoughts	59
	Infernal Monologue	
13.	The Blame Game	63
	On Stoic Progress	

14. Citizen of the World	65
15. The Stoic Love of Community	69
16. When We Stumble	73
Good Fortune: Episode Eight	
17. Physical Exercises	79
Good Fortune: Episode Ten	
18. Uprooting Fear	87
Good Fortune: Episode Eleven	
19. The Stoic Present	95
So Slender an Object	
20. Stoics vs Obstacles and Uncertainty	97
21. Frightened of Change	101
Good Fortune: Episode Twelve	
22. Death and an Epitaph For Ourselves	109
Good Fortune: Episode Thirteen	
23. On Stoic Authority	115
You Shouldn't Eat That	
24. A Wish for Your Good Fortune	119
Good Fortune Episodes	121
Questions Asked and Answered	123
Recommended Resources	125

The Good Fortune Handbook

Hi, I'm Matt Van Natta, the creator of the Stoic podcast *Good Fortune* and writer of the blog, *Immoderate Stoic*. This handbook is a collection of transcripts and articles that are all available for free online. So why am I compiling them? Two reasons. First, it's my hope that the new format will be convenient in its usability. On the internet, no matter how helpful an article may be to people, eventually it gets lost in a back catalog of blog postings. This book will allow the better things to remain visible and therefore, I hope, relevant. Second, currency helps my project keep going. I've had multiple people request to monetarily support my work. I've investigated a variety of ways to do so, but so far I haven't found a method that feels right for what I want *Immoderate Stoic* to be. I feel better about accepting funds when I'm handing you something that is yours (even if that something is digital). Whatever funds I receive from this handbook will help keep *Immoderate Stoic* up and running. Any additional money will help give me breathing room to create a new project I've been slowly pecking away at; a book of original content that aims to help people live out practical Stoicism.

So how to use this book?

The transcripts and articles within this handbook have been ordered thematically, in the hope that anyone who reads from page one until the end will not stumble over too many jarring topic shifts. For readers who are looking for specific episodes of the podcast, *Good Fortune*, an appendix offers an ordering from One to Thirteen. There is also a list of articles by publishing date, and a compendium of questions that allows one to jump to specific topics throughout the book. This handbook is meant as a supplement for people who practice Stoicism daily. As such, it assumes a basic level of understanding of the Stoic philosophy. If you require a basic tutorial, I suggest heading to the Resources section of this book.

Creating *Good Fortune* has enriched my understanding of Stoicism and, more importantly, solidified my practice. I certainly hope that this book proves useful to you as well.

1

What is Stoicism?

> No school has more goodness and gentleness; none has more love for human beings, nor more attention to the common good. The goal which it assigns to us is to be useful, to help others, and to take care, not only of ourselves, but of everyone in general and of each one in particular.
> (On Clemency 3:3)

What is Stoicism?
Stoicism is a practical philosophy that aims to help us live well. As Stoics, we learn to focus on what is in our power. We ask ourselves, "What can we do to create a good life, no matter the circumstances we find ourselves in? What is required of us as human beings and what prevents us from living up to our full potential?" Consistent Stoic practice increases our resilience, contentment, joy, and gives us the boldness necessary to tackle the tasks presented to us in life.

Stoics believe we all have the ability to live a flourishing life, and that such a life requires effort
Stoicism says we should, "live according to nature." I'm not fond of the phrase, because it requires way too much unpacking. To Stoics, our nature is not 'whatever feels right' or 'whatever comes easy.' To us, living naturally means taking actions that allow us to flourish. We're looking for a way to be our best possible selves. Stoicism claims that humans are rational, social beings. Therefore, our nature is to use our rational mind for the benefit of ourselves and our society.

The Good Fortune Handbook

Stoics believe a virtuous life is fully sufficient for happiness

Stoics believe that if you are thinking clearly and acting properly, you can be joyful despite outer circumstances. One person can be content while being deathly ill, whereas another is miserable while in peak health; it's how we choose to see the world that matters. Stoics work to see the world differently. We concentrate our efforts on our own judgments and actions, the things we control, so that we know we did our best despite what fortune brings us.

About Stoic Virtue and the Disciplines

We Stoics explain Virtue thorough the perspectives of Justice, Wisdom, Temperance, and Courage. Our claim is, if you orient yourself to life using these four perspectives as a guide, you'll be taking the best possible path through life.

Along with the Virtues, we have three Disciplines; Assent, Desire, and Action. The Discipline of Assent requires us to be mindful of our judgments at all times. The Discipline of Desire asks us to accept our present circumstances. We do not do this to be passive, but we apply our agency towards things we can truly control, without wasting effort on anything else. The Discipline of Action has to do with our love of humanity and the world. Recognizing that we are social beings, Stoicism requires us to act for the common good. The wide variety of Stoic practices, ancient and modern, stem from these Disciplines which attempt to build up and internalize our understanding of Virtue so that we can live a flourishing life.

2

A Podcast's Introduction

Good Fortune: Episode One

Things don't always go according to plan....
    Hi. This is *Good Fortune* and I'm your host, Matt Van Natta. Today's questions:

- Why *Good Fortune* and what's with that raven?
- Stoic podcast, huh, well what sort of Stoic podcast?
- And finally, I want a boisterous crowd to shut up and go away, how can Stoicism help me with this?

Alright, let's get started!

Why Good Fortune and what's with that raven?
So this is it, episode one of a new Stoic podcast. Once again, I'm Matt Van Natta and I started blogging at *ImmoderateStoic.com* in 2012, just a year after I started practicing Stoicism in earnest. Since then, my writing has been featured in a variety of places including the websites of *Stoicism* Today and *The Spiritual Naturalist Society*. *Stoicism Today* also included me in their book of *Selected Writings*. Additionally, I'm a co-host of the Stoic podcast, *Painted Porch*. I'm also a husband, a father, and a newly minted Oregonian. I just got my driver's license this week.
    So why title this project *Good Fortune*? It comes from a favorite Stoic quote. The Roman emperor Marcus Aurelius was a practicing Stoic. He kept a personal journal about that journey and it has stayed with us until this very day. It's usually titled simply, *Meditations*. In *Meditations*

Aurelius says, "Misfortune, born nobly, is good fortune." To Stoics, there isn't really any bad or good fortune in the world, what happens is simply what happened. It's our personal judgments about events that make things appear good or bad. Aurelius wanted to stop judging events and, instead, judge his own response to events. Would he shut down at the first sign of an obstacle, or adapt and press on? Would he waste his life fearing events that were out of his control, or focus on living with excellence no matter what came his way? "Misfortune, born nobly is good fortune." It's a very short phrase that illustrates an important facet of the Stoic view of life. I picked the title *Good Fortune* because this podcast will be focused on understanding and applying the Stoic orientation to life, so that each of us can learn to live in a state of constant good fortune.

I promised I'd explain the raven as well. I stared at that raven so much during the past months I feel it deserves a name, maybe I'll call her Fortuna? Anyway, the raven is there because ravens are often considered ill omens. The ancient Stoics believed in omens and divination. There are a variety of reasons they took this view, too many to go into right now. Let's just accept that the Stoics believed that certain signs could lead us to knowledge of what was to come. In the *Enchirideon*, which is a handbook composed of notes from the Stoic teacher Epictetus' lectures, Chapter 18 specifically addresses omens and ravens. It ends saying, "…but for me every portent is favorable, if I so wish; for whatever the outcome be, it is within my power to derive benefit from it." So omens were neither good or bad. They're just road signs for life. No matter the signs, how we travel the road remains up to us. You can see how closely aligned Chapter 18 is with Marcus Aurelius' point of view.

Let me be clear, I don't believe in divination and we will not be reading the stars on this podcast. I enjoy the sentiment expressed in Chapter 18 even though I don't make my decisions based on what birds do or do not do in my presence.

Enough about all that. What sort of Stoic podcast is this? Well, I won't be doing interviews. If you want those listen to *Painted Porch* over at *PaintedPorch.org*, there's great stuff there. As a co-host, I'm biased, but I'm right. I will also be avoiding delving deep into the nooks and crannies of Stoic philosophy. There will be explanations of Stoic thinking, and at times some technical points will most likely be made, but *Good Fortune* is about practical, actionable Stoicism. My ideal is that every episode clearly elaborates on the Stoic view of the world. How do we view insults? What's the proper reaction to a traffic jam? Should I be politically active? I want to uncover the Stoic view or views of everyday events and follow up with practices that can help us adopt and maintain that Stoic outlook.

Now, an offshoot of the "what sort of Stoic podcast" question is "what sort of Stoicism" is going to be presented? My goal is to be accessible to anyone with an interest in Stoicism. In fact, you might just be interested in general self-help, lifehacking sort of stuff. I will always be speaking about Stoicism, as a Stoic, but all ears are welcome. And your voice is welcome too, through *ImmoderateStoic.com* as well as social media. So, what kind of Stoicism will be presented here? Here's a description of Stoicism penned (quilled?) by the Roman Stoic, Seneca, "No school has more goodness and gentleness; none has more love for human beings, nor more attention to the common good. The goal which it assigns to us is to be useful, to help others, and to take care, not only of ourselves, but of everyone in general and of each one in particular." Stoicism, properly practiced, lifts people up and draws them closer together. That's the Stoicism I hope to understand better and practice daily and that is the Stoicism I will be presenting here.

I also want to keep things short. So I think I've said enough about what *Good Fortune* is meant to be, let's move on to the final question.

I want a boisterous crowd to shut up and go away, how can Stoicism help me with this?

Ah the crowd…how often you have annoyed me. Some of you may be blessed with a natural love of humanity at its loudest and most tightly packed. The rest of you have probably shared my dismay when surrounded by an unexpected throng of revelers. Well, I am pleased to report that Stoicism offers a solution, however, like most every Stoic solution, it involves a change, not in others, but within ourselves.

When you're alone you should call this condition tranquility and freedom, and think of yourself like the gods; and when you are with many, you shouldn't call it a crowd, or trouble, or uneasiness, but *festival* and company, and contentedly accept it.

So you can see what Epictetus did there, basically he switched out some words; but it's not simply wordplay! He's re-framing the situation from a random crowd to a festival. The Festival Mindset is an idea that is very important to me because I've been very anxious in my life, especially in social situations, and I've found this one word, *festival*, to be supremely important in overcoming a lot of that anxiety. Don't think that Epictetus is just advocating for wordplay. Within the word festival is an entire mindset that, if embraced, really does make dealing with people easier. We've all been to a festival that we've wanted to go to; a party, a concert, somewhere where we were among our people, we were doing what we wanted to do, and it was fun. The fact is, when we're at those sort of events we tend to give a lot of grace to the people around us. The loudness doesn't seem as loud, or at least as annoying, the jostling is taken in stride, whatever it is that's going on, if it's in the spirit of the festival, great! The problem, of course, is when we're somewhere we don't want to be or weren't expecting to be. I'll tell you that I don't watch a lot of American football, never have. Because of that, it's so far removed from my thinking process that it never dawns on me that I might go out at night to a place that is showing a football game and will be crowded and loud. Now, that's all on me. It's not hard to know what night football's happening and it's not hard to know which of the places I visit have multiple televisions. But that doesn't change the fact that it's pretty easy to get annoyed at people when they are interrupting whatever it is that you want to do. That's where the Festival mindset comes in.

I have, for the past couple of years, made it a point to say rather consistently, "festival," the actual word, to myself whenever I'm out in a crowd. I have a story I've used to illustrate this in the past. For whatever reason, I have a habit of going out to read at bars; which is a little weird. I mean, I just want a cocktail and a nice book, but it can look odd to be sitting at a bar where everyone else is having fun and be the one flipping through a book. But whatever, I'm used to being considered weird and I've given up long ago on what other people think about that. But still, I'm going to a loud place to do something that is inherently quiet.

So I'm at a bar with book in hand, sat down to order my cocktail, and couldn't help by notice a particularly loud party going on behind me. It didn't annoy me. As I said, I've gotten pretty good at putting myself in the right mindset before going out but it was very loud and distracting; so much so that the bartender began coming up and telling patrons a little bit about that group. When he came around to me he said, "Hey buddy, just so you know, the table behind you is part of an engagement party." Now I was already in a good mood, but that context was important. It made people seem less obnoxious that they were celebrating an engagement than if they were just really drunk and really loud.

Now this particular event stuck in my head because a little bit latter a couple came into the bar and sat next to me and they were obviously distracted by the group behind us. The guy would turn and stare people down and then the woman would do the same. Then they would sort of whisper to each other. They were obviously annoyed. When a natural pause in there conversation came up I turned to them and said, "Hey, just so you know, that's an engagement party back there." And they said…"Oh, that's cool," and for the entire rest of the night it was obvious that the were no longer annoyed by the group!

This is what Epictetus wants us to do in all situations: decide we're at a big party and that everyone around us is in our company and then contentedly accept it. There's another standard Stoic quote, also from Epictetus,

> It is impossible that happiness and yearning for what is not present should ever be united.

If you want it to be quiet when it isn't, you're not going to be content and that's unfortunate because it's possible (at least in most situations) to change your mind about what you want. So one last time, "When you're alone you should call this condition tranquility and freedom, and think of yourself like the gods; and when you are with many, you shouldn't call it a crowd, or trouble, or uneasiness, but festival and company, and contentedly accept it."

3

A Stoic Start to the Day

Good Fortune: Episode Two

Before you can have a Stoic day you need to wake up. And no, I'm not talking about enlightenment. I'm talking about rolling out of bed, preferably on the right side of it.

Hi, I'm Matt Van Natta and this is *Good Fortune*. Today's questions:

- Why shouldn't I sleep the day away?
- How do Stoics prepare for the inevitable frustrations of the day?
- And finally, I have some extra time in the morning, are there any Stoic practices that can help me start the day right?

Alright, let's get started...

Why shouldn't I sleep the day away?

Are you a morning person? I imagine that's helpful, easily waking up during the hours that society prefers you be active. I wouldn't really know. I was a United States Marine and even then I never took to a morning schedule. I just learned that the human brain does not have to be fully awake while running through the desert wearing a heavy pack.

Emperor and Stoic, Marcus Aurelius, may not have been much of a morning person himself. I come to this conclusion because he takes the time to write to himself about Stoic reasons for not sleeping the day away.

In his *Meditations* Book 5, Chapter 1, Aurelius says,

> At dawn, when you have trouble getting out of bed, tell yourself; 'I have to go to work, as a human being. What do I have to complain of, if I'm going to do what I was born for — the things I was brought into this world to do? Or is this what I was created for? To huddle under the blankets and stay warm?–but it's nicer here? So you were born to feel 'nice'? Instead of doing things and experiencing them?

Aurelius continues, and I suggest reading the whole chapter, but I think from the opening lines we can get the gist. The comfort and pleasure of oversleeping isn't really enriching our lives. There's work to be done. The work of human beings. At the end of Chapter 5, the Emperor talks about people who love their work, the artist or writer who forgets to eat because their so wrapped up in their art. As Stoics we should strive to love the work of the human being, the very act of living well, as much as the starving artist loves their art. We should want to wake up.

How do Stoics prepare for the inevitable frustrations of the day?

So we get out of bed and prepare for the day. Maybe you shower, eat breakfast, brush your teeth. Perhaps you have to pack some books for school or a briefcase for work. What do you do to prepare your mind? You're going to get stuck in traffic, deal with a less than pleasant person, get dragged into an hour long meeting that should have been an email. Have you prepared for that?

Stoic writings provide us with a variety of practices that aim to prepare the mind for the day ahead. One such method is premeditation.

You may already know about the Stoic premeditation of evils. Stoics quite famously take time to dwell on difficult things, the loss of a job, the death of a loved one, the Stoic's own death. I am not recommending that you start your day thinking about death and destruction. I'll cover that in a future episode. The premeditations that I would like to focus on are more general in nature: a series of

Stoic maxims that, if repeated in the morning, can prepare us to react stoically to unfortunate events.

In *Meditations* Book 2, Chapter 1, Aurelius reminds himself how to begin the day.

> When you wake up in the morning, tell yourself: The people I deal with today will be meddling, ungrateful, arrogant, dishonest, jealous, and surly. They are like this because they can't tell good from evil. But I have seen the beauty of good, and the ugliness of evil, and have recognized that the wrongdoer has a nature related to my own — not of the same blood or birth, but the same mind, and possessing a share of the divine. And so none of them can hurt me. No one can implicate me in ugliness. Nor can I feel angry at my relative, or hate him. We were born to work together, like feet, hands, and eyes, like the two rows of teeth, upper and lower. To obstruct each other is unnatural. To feel anger at someone, to turn your back on him: these are obstructions.

Sometimes, in discussions of Stoic premeditation, you'll find people who believe the practice is about steeling yourself against the world. They'll read Marcus's words and say, "yep, people are jerks, defend yourself, shields up!" That response is decidedly un-stoic. Aurelius does begin by reminding himself that people are going to be people and that people are often less than at their best. He then reminds himself of a Stoic belief; that bad actions come from bad thinking or, as he puts it, "they can't tell what is good and what is evil." Stoicism claims that every person is doing the best they can with the information they have. That knowledge is meant to allow a Stoic to accept others despite their faults, because they literally don't know better. Aurelius continues that line of reasoning by reminding himself of the Stoic insistence that all human beings are our family and meant to be treated as such. In addition, Aurelius points out that Stoics can not be harmed by the ill actions of others, in that another person's mistake can not cause us to act inappropriately. Others may be, meddling, ungrateful, arrogant, dishonest, jealous and surly, but what of it? We can respond well. The only real harm is being less than our best, that is what keeps us from flourishing, and that harm can't be done to us, it's done by us, to ourselves. After all, if a Stoic uses another person's un-stoic actions as an excuse to act un-stoically...well, that would be ridiculous. Aurelius finishes with two thoughts, first, that humans are born to work together. Stoicism defines humans not only as rational beings but as social ones. A large part of the Stoic virtue *courage* is practiced by being radically humane in the face of an inhumane world. And so the Emperor's final thought is this, "To obstruct each other is unnatural. To feel anger at someone, to turn your back on them: these are obstructions." This last line is not a final shot at the misguided people Aurelius expects to meet during his day, it's an admonition directed towards himself. A reminder to never be an obstruction to others. No matter how many people try to trip a Stoic up, we prepare ourselves to help them on their way.

There is also a premeditation compiled from the work of Seneca. I believe I first came across it in *The Inner Citadel* by Pierre Hadot. Originally I thought Seneca composed this premeditation, but I haven't been able to find it in his writings. However, I have found every line of the meditation in various places within Seneca's works, so I believe this has been cobbled together later to remind Stoics of some important truths. Again, truths best remembered in the morning.

> The wise will start each day with the thought, "Fortune gives us nothing which we can really own." Nothing, whether public or private, is stable; the destinies of men, no less than those of cities, are in a whirl. Whatever structure has been reared by a long sequence of years, at the cost of great toil and through the great kindness of the gods, is scattered and dispersed in a single day. No, he who has said 'a day' has granted too long a postponement to swift misfortune; an hour, an instant of time, suffices for the overthrow of empires. How often have cities in Asia, how often in Achaia, been laid low by a single shock of earthquake? How many towns in Syria, how many in Macedonia, have been swallowed up? How often has this

kind of devastation laid Cyprus in ruins? We live in the middle of things which have all been destined to die. Mortal have you been born, to mortals you have given birth. Reckon on everything, expect everything.

Here we concentrate, not only on people, but on the whims of Fortune. Seneca reminds us that life does not come with guarantees and everything will come to an end. In Stoicism, change is a universal constant. To expect permanence in an ever-changing world is to court disappointment at best. In the *Enchiridion*, Chapter 11, the Stoic teacher Epictetus reminds his students to "never say of anything, "I have lost it" but–"I have returned it."" He advises us to take care of whatever we possess, but not to view it as our own, but as a traveler views a hotel. To begin the day as a Stoic, we prepare ourselves to embrace the world as it truly is, so that we can act meaningfully within it. We can remind ourselves that people may act poorly and events may change our fortunes abruptly, but those challenges can not keep us from being our best selves.

As a modern Stoic teacher, Keith Seddon, once wrote, "We must invest our hopes not in the things that happen, but in our capacities to face them as human beings."

Are there any Stoic practices that can help me start my day right?
I have a favorite visualization technique that has helped me when I've woken up anxious. It's called the View from Above, and I find that it helps put life into a universal context, thereby shrinking my problems down to size. If you have ten...twenty minutes to set aside in the morning, this practice might be for you.

The View from Above, in short, consists in mentally placing yourself high above the earth, a literal view from above, so as to gaze down on the works of humankind and say, hmm...that's all, what am I so worried about?

In her book, *Stoic Spiritual Exercises,* Elene Buzare tells us that,

> This exercise is a good one to learn for situating things within the immensity of the Universe and the totality of

Nature, without the false prestige lent to them by our human passions and conventions...The 'view from above' should change our judgments on things concerning luxury, power, war, borders and the worries of everyday life, whether these occur within our families, at work or elsewhere, by re-situating them within the immensity of the cosmos and the vastness of human experience.

Indeed, when we look at things from the perspective of the Cosmos, those things which do not depend on us, and which Stoics call 'indifferents', are brought back to their true proportions...This exercise, then, should also help us contemplate how foolish most of our actions are, and remind us of the imminence of death...and the urgency of our practice!

The modern Stoic writer Donald Robertson shares a wonderful version of this practice on his website, which I will link to in the show notes. So as not to repeat him, I will share a similar meditation, one written by Carl Sagan when he wrote about a picture of the Earth taken from 4 billion miles away, where our Earth is just a pixel of blue.

"Look again at that dot. That's here. That's home. That's us. On it everyone you love, everyone you know, everyone you ever heard of, every human being who ever was, lived out their lives. The aggregate of our joy and suffering, thousands of confident religions, ideologies, and economic doctrines, every hunter and forager, every hero and coward, every creator and destroyer of civilization, every king and peasant, every young couple in love, every mother and father, hopeful child, inventor and explorer, every teacher of morals, every corrupt politician, every "superstar," every "supreme leader," every saint and sinner in the history of our species lived there—on a mote of dust suspended in a sunbeam.

The Earth is a very small stage in a vast cosmic arena. Think of the rivers of blood spilled by all those generals and emperors so that, in glory and triumph, they could become the momentary masters of a fraction of a dot. Think of the endless cruelties visited by the inhabitants of one corner of this pixel on the scarcely distinguishable inhabitants of some other corner, how frequent their misunderstandings, how eager they are to kill one another, how fervent their hatreds.

Our posturings, our imagined self-importance, the delusion that we have some privileged position in the Universe, are challenged by this point of pale light. Our planet is a lonely speck in the great enveloping cosmic dark. In our obscurity, in all this vastness, there is no hint that help will come from elsewhere to save us from ourselves.

The Earth is the only world known so far to harbor life. There is nowhere else, at least in the near future, to which our species could migrate. Visit, yes. Settle, not yet. Like it or not, for the moment the Earth is where we make our stand.

It has been said that astronomy is a humbling and character-building experience. There is perhaps no better demonstration of the folly of human conceits than this distant image of our tiny world. To me, it underscores our responsibility to deal more kindly with one another, and to preserve and cherish the pale blue dot, the only home we've ever known."

Carl Sagan was not, to my knowledge, a practicing Stoic, but he certainly had a universal perspective. If you have some time in the morning, take the time to remind yourself that you and none of the things around you are the center of the universe, but you are a part of it.

4

A Stoic End to the Day

Good Fortune: Episode Five

So we wake up and begin the day as Stoics. We prepare ourselves for the inconveniences of life with a Morning Meditation, we strive to pay attention to our thoughts throughout the day and we divide events into those that we do and do not control…eventually, the sun sets, we get ready to sleep until another day begins. How did we do? Did we succeed at the day we just lived? Did we fail? Most likely we did a bit of both. Should we just go to sleep and leave the past in the past, or should we learn lessons from the day, celebrate our successes and admonish ourselves for our faults? How does a Stoic end the day?

Hi. I'm Matt Van Natta and this is *Good Fortune*. Today's questions:

- Is there a Stoic way to go to sleep?
- Is it possible to do Stoic exercises incorrectly?

And finally, a bonus means of applying today's exercise, this one aimed at parents. All right, let's get started.

Is there a Stoic way to go to sleep?

Of course there is, those ancient Stoics had opinions about pretty much everything. In the case of preparing to sleep, Stoics call on a practice that predates Stoicism itself. This exercise is often called the Evening Meditation, though I prefer the term Retrospective Mediation. Variations of the Evening Meditation are found in Seneca's works and in Epictetus's *Discourses*. In *Discourses* Book 3, Chapter 10, Line 3, we find Epictetus quoting a Pythagorean practice,

> Do not let sleep fall upon your soft eyes
> Before you have gone over each act of your day three times:
> Where have I failed? At what have I succeeded? What duty have I omitted?
> Begin here , and continue the examination. After this
> Find fault with what was badly done, and rejoice in what was good.

The Retrospective Meditation is meant to assist us in learning from the life we're living. No matter how well we prepare for the day, beginning our morning with the View from Above and girding our minds like Aurelius recommends in his *Meditations*, we will stumble. We may notice that we've screwed up, but we might be oblivious to it. Perhaps the reason the meeting didn't go well is because I was the obstinate jerk, not my co-worker like I had convinced myself at the time. When do we take the time to learn from our mistakes? Because moving on is not the same as learning. If I am put in the same situation, will I fail again, or will I flourish?

We find Seneca's mention of Retrospective Meditation in his work titled *On Anger*. I'll quote from the translation used in Elen Buzare's excellent book *Stoic Spiritual Exercises*.

> [One's mind] should be summoned each day to give account of itself. Sextius used to do this. At the day's end, when he had retired for the night, he would interrogate his mind: 'What ailment of yours have you cured today? What failing have you resisted? Where can you show improvement?...
>
> Could anything be finer than this habit of sifting through the whole day? Think of the sleep that follows the self-examination! How calm, deep, unimpeded it must be, when the mind has been praised or admonished and – its own sentinel and censor – has taken stock secretly of its own habits.

I like the promise of better sleep. I've had many an anxious night in my own life, so I appreciate the calm sleep that comes with being at peace with oneself. Now here's the part where I admit that I often skip my Evening Meditation. Which is ridiculous because I can attest to the fact that it is a powerful exercise that, at least for me, truly delivers. It's purely a lack of discipline on my part that has kept me from practicing nightly. That said, working on this episode has gotten me back on track and I'm happy that it has.

In both Retrospective Meditations, we find three questions.

In Epictetus: Where have I failed? At what have I succeeded? What duty have I omitted?

In Seneca: What ailment of yours have you cured today? What failing have you resisted? Where can you show improvement?

Each of these sets of questions requires radical honesty with ourselves if they're to be effective. I should hope we can all be bold enough to be that honest, after all, Seneca mentions that our mind takes stock secretly of its own habits. There's no requirement to share anything with the world, other than more compassionate and rational actions as we improve ourselves.

Is it possible to do the Stoic evening meditation, or really, any Stoic meditation, wrong?

Yes. Stoic exercises can be done incorrectly. Improper Stoic practices stem from a Chicken and the Egg problem. In order to exercise Stoicism properly, we have to understand the Stoic worldview, but taking in that worldview requires the practice...and so on and so forth. Many of the ancient Stoics had the benefit of instruction from teachers; teachers who could check their mental form the same way a trainer can correct the form of an athlete. Modern Stoics have it harder. Many of us pick up a practice here and there, and don't get to see how the practice fits into the whole of Stoic teaching until much later in our journey. This is one of the reasons I harp on the expected outcomes of a Stoic life. Quotes like this one from Seneca,

> No school has more goodness and gentleness; none has more love for human beings, nor more attention to the

> common good. The goal which it assigns to us is to be useful, to help others, and to take care, not only of ourselves, but of everyone in general and of each one in particular.

or definitions like this one from Marcus Aurelius:

> Nothing should be called good that fails to enlarge our humanity.

If we see clearly what the Stoic life is said to be, but can find no way that a certain practice could lead to that place, then either the Stoics are simply wrong, or our thinking is wrong concerning that Stoic practice.

The primary pitfall concerning the Evening or Retrospective Meditation is this: believing that clearly seeing and admonishing ourselves for our failures is the same thing as wallowing in those failures. Stoicism never recommends beating ourselves up for our faults. Stoics seek to overcome our weaknesses, not dwell on them forever.

I will be linking to a *Stoicism Today* article by Donald Robertson titled, *The Evening Meditation: Some Reflections*. I recommend reviewing it for more about the Retrospective Meditation. At one point Donald says,

> Seneca describes his self-examination as if it were analogous to a defendant appearing in court. It's important not to allow this to turn into a kind of morbid rumination or worry. I think there's perhaps just a knack to keeping it constructive that comes with experience. Another observation I'd make that might help Stoics manage this is that, of course, the events being reviewed, as they are in the past, are all in the domain of things outside of your control and therefore, I assume, "indifferent" in the Stoic sense of the word. Hence, there's not much point worrying about them. The most we can do is learn from them.

He is exactly right. We can't repair our mistakes, but we can fix what ails us so that we don't make that mistake again.

Donald Robertson's quote mentions Seneca's courtroom version of the Evening Meditation. I think it's worth looking at, as an example of how to practice this discipline.

> Every day I plead my cause before the bar of myself. When the light has been removed from sight, and my wife, long aware of my habit, has become silent, I scan the whole of my day and retrace all my deeds and words. I conceal nothing from myself, I omit nothing. For why should I shrink from any of my mistakes, when I may commune thus with myself? 'See that you never do that again. I will pardon you this time. In that dispute, you spoke too offensively; after this don't have encounters with ignorant people; those who have never learned do not want to learn. You reproved that man more frankly than you ought, and consequently you have not so much mended him as offended him. In the future, consider not only the truth of what you say, but also whether the man to whom you are speaking can endure the truth. A good man accepts reproof gladly, the worse a man is the more bitterly he resents it.

That's all I have to share concerning the standard use of the Retrospective Meditation, but I want to present an alternative use that I wrote about on *ImmoderateStoic.com* some time back.

A few years ago I came across an article on how to properly praise children. The article sited actual child development research, it wasn't simply a blog post concerning a parent's gut feelings. I related the research, done by a Professor Dweck, to a variety of Stoic beliefs and at the end I found that the Retrospective Meditation actually paired well with the Professor's recommendations. In the article I read, Professor Dweck said she, "believes families should sit around the dinner table discussing the day's struggles and new strategies for attacking the problem. In life no one can be perfect, and learning to view little failures as learning experiences, or opportunities to grow could be the most valuable lesson of all."

As Stoic parents, we can practice this idea and grow in our philosophy while doing so. I suggest that as we gather our family around a meal, where we probably already ask, "what did you do today?" we add the questions, "What did you succeed at and struggle with today?" and "What needs to be done tomorrow?" We can share in the triumphs of our children's day. We can share our own challenges so that our children understand that struggle is to be expected. We can plan together, as a family, our strategies to overcome obstacles big and small. In doing so, we build an understanding of, and appreciation for, the process of learning in our children (and ourselves) and they will be stronger for it. Like the ancient Stoics, we can choose to praise those things that lead to wisdom and, in doing so, we will help our children thrive.

5

Attention is Fundamental

Good Fortune: Episode Three

Yesterday I was crossing the Ross Island Bridge and the person ahead of me was driving like a real idiot. I spent a few moments remarking on this fact, to myself, when I was reminded of Marcus Aurelius's premeditation, the one I mentioned just last episode. I had neglected to start my day by reminding myself that people were going to act selfishly, rudely, etcetera. It took the mornings first act of actual rudeness to bring my thoughts back into focus. I am happy to report that that sudden irritation was soothed by Stoic thoughts but, of course, that is not the ideal. I should have begun my day by composing my thoughts. Or even better, my mind should be so rooted in a Stoic orientation that I would never think to BE annoyed by something as small as a sudden lane change or whatever. But how can I think Stoically with that level of consistency?

Hi. I'm Matt Van Natta and this is Good Fortune. Today's questions:

- How hard is it to think like a Stoic?
- How do we develop a consistent Stoic orientation towards the world?
- And finally, What sort of practice can help us keep a constant Stoic attitude in life?

Alright, let's get started…

How hard is it to think like a Stoic?

I'm going to let the ancient teacher Musonius Rufus address this point. Musonius was the head of the Stoic school in his day. We don't have access to much of Musonius's teachings, history has erased all but a few of his works, but what we do have is interesting and enlightening.

For example, his thoughts on Stoic practice,

> Therefore practicing each virtue always must follow learning the lessons appropriate to it, or it is pointless for us to learn about it. The person who claims to be studying philosophy must practice it even more diligently than the person who aspires to the art of medicine or some similar skill, inasmuch as philosophy is more important and harder to grasp than any other pursuit. People who study skills other than philosophy have not been previously corrupted in their souls by learning things contrary to what they are about to learn, but people who attempt to study philosophy, since they have been already in the midst of much corruption and are filled with evil, pursue virtue in such a condition that they need even more practice in it.

We can hope that a woman training to become a surgeon has not been performing amateur surgeries on the side prior to attending medical school. Instead, she gets to start her schooling using the proper tools to learn the most appropriate technique until she has mastered the skills necessary to practice medicine. The school of philosophy is meant to give us the skill to see the world clearly but we have all been taking in and judging the events of life since drawing our first breath. We have already spent decades as untrained amateurs; patching our faults up with duct tape and using a wrench to pound in nails. Stoicism provides us with new tools and techniques for shaping our thoughts and actions but we humans are very attached to our old ways. So learning to live stoically is as hard as breaking a habit… or beginning a better one. Except we're attempting to break every bad habit, including those we don't yet recognize in ourselves. If we're going to have any hope of real progress towards Stoic goals, if we're going to train ourselves to think differently, we're going to have to learn to pay attention.

Attention is Fundemental   25

How do we develop a consistent Stoic orientation to the world?

We begin by paying attention. Pierre Hadot, in his book *The Inner Citadel*, says this:

> Attention is the fundamental Stoic spiritual attitude. It is a continuous vigilance and presence of mind, self-consciousness which never sleeps, and a constant tension of the spirit. Thanks to this attitude, the philosopher is fully aware of what he does at each instant, and he wills his actions fully.

I agree with Hadot that attention is foundational to the Stoic mind. Attention paid, not simply to the world around us, but even more importantly to *our own* thoughts and feelings. The Stoic aim is to lead a flourishing life. We do this by dismantling any mental habits that lead us astray and replacing them with a more effective understanding of the world; one that leads to virtuous, and therefore powerful, actions.

I am often drawn to Hadot's phrase, "a constant tension of the spirit." It sounds exhausting, doesn't it? Well, that shouldn't surprise us. The Stoic philosophy is not complete on the page, it only exists in practice. And exercise is always strenuous if it's at all useful. Or to return to Musonius's love of medical examples, "The philosopher's school is a doctor's office, you must leave not pleased but pained." If we are going to flourish in life, we have to cut out the bad and build up the good.

What sort of philosophical practice can help us keep a constant Stoic attitude in life?

The short answer is all of them. Look at any of the exercises we've already covered and it's obvious that attention underlies them all. Before we can remind ourselves that we are at a festival, instead of stuck in a crowd, we have to have the presence of mind to realize the need for that mental realignment. Before I can stay calm and relaxed in traffic, I have to be conscious enough of my own thoughts to realize that I'm losing myself in petty mental bickering.

The Stoic mindset, what Hadot calls the "Stoic spiritual attitude," is explained in Book 9, Chapter 6 of *Meditations* where Marcus Aurelius says,

> Here is what is enough for you:
> 1. the judgment you are bringing to bear at this moment upon reality, as long as it is objective.
> 2. the action you are carrying out at this moment, as long as it is accomplished in the service of the human community; and
> 3. the inner disposition in which you find yourself at this moment, as long as it is a disposition of joy in the face of the conjunction of events caused by extraneous causality.

We pay attention to our own responses to the present moment, because the present is all we have. The present moment is the only place that we can effect change in our lives or in the world.

As the Roman Stoic Seneca said it, "These two things must be cut away: fear of the future, and the memory of past sufferings. The latter no longer concern me, and the future does not concern me yet."

So yes, every Stoic practice requires and bolsters our attention but of course, I am not going to leave you without a particular Stoic discipline for the week. Marcus Aurelius writes of a method that can serve us well, this exercise, sometimes referred to as *physical definition*, requires us to pay attention to both the external world and our inner judgments concerning the world.

He expresses the art of physical definition most clearly in the beginning of *Meditations* 3:11;

> To the stand-bys above, add this one: always to define whatever it is that we perceive — to trace its outline — so that we can see what it really is, its substance. Stripped bare. As a whole. Unmodified. And to call it by its name –the thing itself and its components, to which it will eventually return. Nothing is so conductive to spiritual growth as this capacity for logical and accurate analysis of everything that happens to us. To look at it in such a way that we understand what need it fulfills, and in what kind of world.

And its value to the world as a whole and to man in particular...

What is it — this thing that now forces itself on my notice? What is it made up of? How long was it designed to last? And what qualities do I need to bring to bear on it — tranquility, courage, honesty, trustworthiness, straightforwardness, independence or what?"

Here we try to see whatever concerns us as it truly is. Now, I don't want to stumble into never-ending debates concerning objectivity/subjectivity and the like. Here, we can say that seeing something as it truly is entails observing its value in terms of promoting a flourishing world and then deciding what actions we must take in light of that value.

In another chapter of the meditations, Emperor Aurelius reminds himself that the meal he is eating is simply a dead fish. Why would he bother? Well, we can find examples within Stoic works, Epictetus' in particular, that speak about putting our social duties during a feast above our basic bodily needs and desires. Marcus Aurelius was the most powerful man in his world. I'm guessing his kitchen staff was pretty talented. Picture this man watching a plate of his favorite herbed fish as it is brought to him so that he can have the first serving before it continues around the banquet. He wants to be a gracious host and he also desires the tasty tasty fish. He could view the meal in terms of misguided values, "it's the best tasting thing in Rome, (I must taste it) the spice mix is worth more that most people's homes, (I deserve it) or I'm the Emperor and I can show my power by eating the whole thing while everyone else salivates."Instead he steps back mentally and says, "this is simply a dead fish, burnt over a flame, with some leaves and twigs thrown on for flavor, am I seriously allowing a dead fish to stand in the way of my better self?"

We can do the same as Emperor Aurelius, step back and give our better nature a fighting chance against the storm of desires that rise up so unthinkingly in the day to day.

The goal of physical definition is to develop a healthy perspective of the world. Really, that's the goal of all Stoic practice; to make our minds sharp, strong, and effective, so that we can live well and help others as we do so.

6

What We Control

Good Fortune: Episode Four

"Some things are under our control, while others are not under our control." That is the famous first line from the *Enchiridion* of Epictetus. It clearly lays out the dichotomy of control, a core means of thinking as a Stoic. Before we can act well, it's important to understand what we can effect, otherwise we may spin our wheels but go nowhere. So what is under our control? And what are the benefits of focusing our energies entirely on those things?

Hi. I'm Matt Van Natta and this is Good Fortune. Today's questions:

- How can I become invincible?
- How can we internalize what is under our control?
- And finally, If Stoic invincibility is achievable, what would that life look like?

All right, let's get started...

How can I become invincible?

That's an odd starting question, right? How did I get from what is or is not under our control to the concept of invincibility? Well, that's Epictetus's fault. Not too far from line one of the *Enchiridion*, in the same chapter in fact, Epictetus says this,

> but if you suppose only to be your own that which is your own, and what belongs to others such as it really is, then

no one will ever compel you or restrain you. Further, you will find fault with no one and accuse no one. You will do nothing against your will. No one will hurt you, you will have no enemies, and you will not be harmed.

The first chapter of the *Enchiridion* is bold. Just a few lines in, and the head of the Stoic school is claiming that his philosophy can make a person invincible. If I were handed a pamphlet that explained some random group's belief system and paragraph one said, "Follow these teachings and you will have no enemies and will not be harmed," I would stay far away from that group. So assuming Epic isn't a crazy cult leader what could he possibly mean?

Let's return to line one, now with line two for some context.

Some things are under our control, while others are not under our control. Under our control are opinion, choice, desire, aversion, and, in a word, everything that is our own doing; not under our control are our body, our property, reputation, office, and, in a word, everything that is not our own doing.

Everything Epictetus lists as under our control is mental. and he doesn't even include all of our mental life. for instance, you may notice that emotions aren't mentioned. Outside of our control are a much wider variety of things, our property, our reputation, our station in life. All of these things include our participation, of course, but our control of outcomes is limited. Did you notice what I just left off the not-under-our-control list? The body. Epictetus lists our own body as outside of our control. His list leads with the body and he almost doesn't need to follow up with property, reputation, and so forth. If my arm is not under my control, Stoically speaking, I'm guessing anything at an arm's length is even less in my sphere of influence. So, I find that Epictetus effectively gets across the idea that Stoicism considers only the mental life, our opinions, choices, desires, and aversions, to be under our complete control. What does that mean? Are we to draw so completely into ourselves that nothing outside of our own thoughts matters? Surely not. Stoics have always been active individuals, often real political animals.

No. We are supposed to engage with the world, but we are meant to do so effectively. You've probably heard the phrase, "Resentment is like drinking poison and expecting someone else to die"? Focusing our mental energy on things outside of our control tends to be ineffective in just this way.

The Stoic claim is that if we focus on holding intelligent opinions, making wise choices, desiring worthy things, and avoiding, not externals, like struggle, pain, and other uncomfortable situations, but instead avoid only those things that make us less virtuous, if we do that, our every action will be victorious because, even if the outcome is less than perfect, we will still have won because we obtained our goal; that of taking the best action possible while remaining true to our humanity.

How can we internalize what is under our control?

Understanding that our opinions, choices, desires, and aversions are under our control does not automatically make those things healthy. We have to learn what to choose, what to desire, but before all that, we have to learn how to examine our mind and challenge the unhealthy thoughts that reside there.

In Stoicism, there is a practice called **suspension of judgment**. this is a constant practice, a way of thinking, not just something we are to do at the end of the day. The basic idea is to pause and examine our thoughts to see if they are true. Some thoughts are more worthy of examination than others, of course. Let's say we're traveling by plane and have hit some severe turbulence. The thought, "I am on a plane," doesn't really require examination. Nor does the thought, "the plane is experiencing turbulence." But what if you think, "We're all going to die?" That is quite an opinion, one that may elicit strong emotions and irrational actions...it is worth examining. If a thought like that bubbles up. Stop. Acknowledge it. It has already happened, after all. no need to suppress it. Instead challenge it. Realize that thinking something isn't the same as approving of it. In Stoicism we call this *withholding assent*.

There's a good chance that you've seen at least one of the Marvel movies that have Tony Stark, a.k.a Iron Man in them. If Tony Stark is in a movie, it's inevitable that he will interact with a hologram. Usually he's looking at the schematics of some sort of machine. He'll reach into the hologram and pluck out a piece of it to examine more closely. It's a cool effect and it's my personal visual when I examine my thoughts. I pick the thought in question out of my head and strip it into its parts. Am I on a plane? Yes. Is there turbulence? That checks out too. Am I going to die? How could I possibly know that? I may feel that I'm going to die, but that state of mind is built on imagination, not truth. I refuse to assent to it. No seal of approval for you thought!

There's another aspect of the thought I need to evaluate. Even if it were true, does it concern me? Meaning: is the thought about something I control? Well, I have pretty much zero effect on whether or not a plane I'm on is going to crash. I can fasten a seat belt, put up my tray, and place my seat in an upright position, but none of that keeps a plane in the sky.

Back to the idea behind "resentment is like drinking poison and expecting someone else to die." What am I getting out of fretting over the state of the airplane? Not peace of mind. So am I trading that peace of mind in exchange for something more desirable? Does my fretting keep the plane in the sky? That would be great, but that's not how the universe works. So I'm getting nothing out of the deal. All I am doing is making myself useless to myself, and also to others if there were an actual crisis.

So how should I think, if I could be the best Stoic I could possible be?

One more Epictetus quote:

> I will show the nerves of a philosopher. "What nerves are these?" A desire never disappointed, an aversion which never falls on that which it would avoid, a proper pursuit, a diligent purpose, an assent which is not rash. These you shall see.

A desire never disappointed: If my desire is based on never experiencing crisis, or never dying, I'm going to be disappointed constantly and then, in my last moments, disappointed finally. If I

What We Control 33

desire to live well, in the present moment, and thrive up until my final moment? That's possible, but I have to stop investing in things I don't control.

An aversion which never falls on that which it would avoid: Again, seeking to avoid struggle, crisis, or death is a fools errand. Seeking to avoid our worst selves, that's possible if we dig in and do the work.

A proper pursuit, a diligent purpose, an assent which is not rash. Aim for these outcomes and our mind will become a tool for change in the world.

So, since I just had us falling out of the sky for 5 minutes, a recap:
Suspend you judgement
Pause and examine your thoughts
Is it provably true and, even if it is,
Is it within your control?
However it all plays out, show the nerves of a philosopher.

If invincibility were possible, what would that life look like?

I saved this for last because I don't want anyone to leave with the idea that advocating for a Stoically self-controlled mind is a call to live a self-centered life.

Chapter 1 of the *Enchiridion* lays out the dichotomy of control as a concept. But what does the life of a Stoic practicing that dichotomy look like? For that, we can turn to Marcus Aurelius. In Book 12 of his *Meditations*, Chapter 3 says this:

> Your three components: body, breath, mind. Two are yours in trust; to the third alone you have clear title.
>
> If you can cut yourself – your mind – free of what other people do and say, of what you've said or done, of the things that you are afraid will happen, the impositions of the body that contains you and the breath within, and what the whirling chaos sweeps in from outside, so that the mind is freed from fate, brought to clarity, and lives life on its own recognizance – doing what's right, accepting what happens, and speaking the truth–
>
> If you can cut free of impressions that cling to the mind,

free of the future and the past – can make yourself, as Empedocles says, "a sphere rejoicing in its perfect stillness,' and concentrate on living what can be lived (which means the present)…then you can spend the time you have left in tranquility. And in kindness. And at peace with the spirit within you.

Here we find a Stoic reminding himself to put his energies into what he can control. What is he "cutting away'? what other people do and say, what *he* has said and done in the past, fear of the future, weaknesses of the body, and the whirling chaos that sweeps in from outside. What does he expect to get from this? Personal happiness despite the world's pain? No. The mind is freed from fate, brought to clarity to live life on its own recognizance which means and again I quote, "doing what is right, accepting what happens, and speaking the truth."

If you care that other people oppose you. If you bend to your own past failures or cringe from imaginary thoughts about the future you will not live a life of justice, or of courage and you certainly won't thrive. You will stumble, bend, and break under the pressure of the world. Or worse, retire from the world to build yourself a cocoon of safety without real regard for others. Stoicism wants to free us to be an unstoppable force, immovable object be damned. We can do what is right, accept the consequences, and continue speaking the truth. We can have the nerves of a philosopher.

7

Handling Distressing News

Good Fortune: Episode Six

The news. Whether it's delivered by a concerned friend, a gossiping co-worker, or a 24 hour television station, difficult news is never far away. Here in the United States, in a little over a week, we've seen murders, watched those deaths effect the beginnings of, at least symbolic, change. And as symbols of man's inhumanity to man come down off of flagpoles, we've also seen a real victory concerning equality under the law and human dignity. With all that going on we hear about more personal things, potential layoffs at our business, a friend who's seriously ill, your favorite player was traded to a different team. The news comes in fast and never seems to leave us alone. What's a Stoic to do?

Hi, I'm Matt Van Natta and this is Good Fortune. Today's questions:

- How are Stoics meant to react to news, particularly the 'bad' kind?
- Stoics use the term 'indifferent' a lot, what do you mean by that?
- Is there anything I can do to feel more in control after receiving bad news?

Alright, let's get started…

How are Stoics meant to react to news, particularly the 'bad' kind?

Whenever some disturbing news is reported to you, you

ought to have ready at hand the following principle: News, on any subject, never falls within the sphere of the moral purpose.

That line is from Epictetus, found in his third book of *Discourses*, Chapter 28. I suppose I can end the episode now, since I've given you the answer. News, on any subject, never falls within the moral purpose. And our moral purpose is where Stoicism tells us to direct all our energy and action. So what do we do with that? Should we never be distressed by the cruelty of the world? Are we meant to shrug at others suffering and simply attend to ourselves? Of course not. But I think we need to unpack some stuff to see why not.

So first we'll allow Epictetus to expand on his own thoughts. After stating that news never falls within the sphere of the moral purpose, he continues,

> Can anyone bring you word that you have been wrong in an assumption or in a desire? -By no means- But he can bring you word that someone is dead. Very well, what is that to you? That someone is speaking ill of you? Very well, what is that to you? That your father is making preparations? Against whom? Surely not against your moral purpose, is it? Why, how can he? But against your paltry body, against your paltry possessions; you are safe, it is not against you.

To understand this argument, we need to look at the Stoic concept of the self and also the preeminence of morality in their worldview. In Stoicism, you are very small and very powerful. What do I mean by that? Well, look at the Father in Epictetus' example. This hypothetical father is taking some sort of action against a Stoic student, perhaps disinheriting him. So this news is quite personal, it's not about a distant war or the misfortunes of a stranger, instead it's literally close to home. Yet the teacher Epictetus says, "what is that to you?" The news may concern your possessions, even your body, but it has nothing to do with YOU. This only makes sense if we understand that in Stoicism, the real you is the ability to choose.

Handling Distressing News 37

I've avoided a lot of Greek terms in these episodes, but today I'm breaking one out: *hegemonikon*, the ruling faculty of the mind. According to the ancient Stoics, the hegemonikon was where all higher cognitive functions and experiences happened. Most importantly, the hegemonikon is the part of us that makes decisions. Also important is that our hegemonikon is considered invincible. Not even Zeus, says Epictetus, can violate our moral will. In Stoicism, this mental complex, the part of us that allows for moral choice, is the real you, the important you, an oh so small aspect of your total humanity, but also the most preeminent and powerful aspect of yourself.

Now, I will take modern neuroscience over early Greek biology every time. The Stoics claimed the hegemonikon resides in the heart, for instance. Still, I think the concept of the hegemonikon, the ruling faculty, is still useful today. Because if you can agree with Stoicism that what really matters isn't what happens in the world, but how you respond to what happens to the world, then you can flourish personally and have a really good chance of helping the world around you flourish as well.

So look again at the student's 'bad' news concerning his father. Epictetus says, "your father is making preparations? Against whom? Surely not against your moral purpose, is it? Why, how can he? But against your paltry body, against your paltry possessions; you are safe, it is not against you." The teacher is saying, yes, something is happening and it could mean the loss of possessions, physical comfort, or even your health. What about this situation can force you to be less than your best? Nothing.

Later in Chapter 28, Epictetus says, "Your father has a certain function, and if he does not perform it, he has destroyed the father in him, the man who loves his offspring, the man of gentleness within him. Do not seek to make him lose anything else on this account. For it never happens that a man goes wrong in one thing, but is injured in another. Again, it is your function to defend yourself firmly, respectfully, without passion. Otherwise, you have destroyed within you the son, the respectful man, the man of honor." This part is important. The son, by Epictetus' logic, can not be harmed by his father's actions, but that does not leave him passive. It allows him to defend himself with a clear head. He remains respectful, does not get angry or depressed or seek revenge, but he does defend himself firmly.

Every episode I end with the Marcus Aurelius quote, "misfortune born nobly is good fortune." Whenever you receive distressing news, remember that line. Can you change what you just heard? No. Can you respond well, both emotionally and with action if possible? Absolutely.

Stoics use the term 'indifferent' a lot, what do you mean by that?

So I just talked on and on about the Stoic concern with moral choice. Now I want to address Stoic indifference. Epictetus claims that, "all news, on any subject falls outside of the sphere of the moral purpose." In Stoic terminology, he just said that all news is indifferent. Indifference comes up a lot in Stoic writings. All those things we don't control, the things I mentioned in Episode 4, body, property, reputation, and so on…these are all indifferent. But as I say that, it's important to understand the Stoic context. Specifically, Stoic indifference means that an object or event does not affect our morality. It is not, it is never, an emotional term. The unloving father in our example is morally indifferent in that nothing he does can force his son to act without virtue. Yet his son would not be acting stoically if he disengaged with his father, wrote him off, and cared nothing for him. As I already mentioned, Epictetus expects that the son will defend himself, but do so respectfully as a proper son, even though his father is not much of a father at all.

So don't fall into the trap of believing Stoic indifference has anything to do with your emotional attachment to or concern for the world at large. Lack of concern for the world is deeply un-Stoic. Marcus Aurelius said his only comfort was moving from one act of service for humanity to another. Epictetus defines right and good actions as those that are *at the same time* affectionate and consistent with reason. Stoic indifference is meant to free us for action. We can say, "no matter what you do, world, I will respond through virtue; justly, wisely, with temperance and courage. No obstacle can keep me from being my best."

Is there anything I can do to feel more in control after hearing bad news?
I often talk about Stoic engagement with the world, that we concentrate on what we control so that our actions are useful and powerful. So how are we supposed to 1. internalize the idea that news does not touch our moral center and 2. engage with that same world in a moral, community-centered way?

In Good Fortune, Episode 3, I spoke of a practice called **Physical Definition**. In this practice, we break down the object or situation that's vexing us into its constituent parts, until we can view it devoid of our preconceptions. Feel free to listen to or read the transcripts of that episode for more information. Today I want to suggest that we can use that same Physical Definition to view disturbing news from a Stoic perspective while also encouraging ourselves to act with purpose within our own sphere of influence.

I agree with the poet Emma Lazarus that "until we are all free, we are none of us free." And so learning of a white supremacist attack in a church, the suppression of peaceful protests in the streets of my country or any other, the denial of human dignity through the letter of the law; all of this weighs on me. It challenges my humanity and asks me 'what, Matt, are you going to do about this?' In answer, I have to first ask, 'what *can* I do about it?' The simple answer to that question is often, 'very little.'

I usually can't fix what was broken. I can't heal the wounded or bring back the dead. I can, perhaps, rage against injustice, but I run the risk of believing my emotions are actions. They are not. I remember reading a psychological study back in college that found the simple act of washing hands could assuage guilt. Individuals can actually 'wash away' their sins. Of course, doing so does nothing to correct the damage that the guilty have done. It simply makes them feel better. Emotions can act like that washing of hands. Righteous indignation can feel important, but it very means little if it doesn't drive us to constructive, righteous actions. So what can we do? In Marcus Aurelius' writings about the practice of Physical Definition, he says this, "What is it — this thing that now forces itself on my notice? What is it made up of? How long was it designed to last? And what qualities do I need to bring to bear on it — tranquility, courage, honesty, trustworthiness, straightforwardness, independence or what?" This is the part of the practice I think we should concentrate on. What qualities of ourselves should we bring to bear on the issue at hand? Have you learned of an injustice? What sort? What would be the proper response, if you had been part of the event? Then, is there a way, here, now, in my own town, my own sphere of influence, that I can work towards a similar justice? We can replace all our impotent despair, disgust, rage, and the like, with potent actions if we are willing to do the work of a virtuous life. So let's get to it.

8

Stoicism and the Blues

> Today I have got out of all trouble, or rather I have cast out all trouble, for it was not outside, but within and in my opinions.
> (Marcus Aurelius)

I had a rough couple of days this week. I've dealt with depression on and off (mostly on) since about the age of twelve. A few days ago, it came back full force. And yes, I know that technically depression needs to stick around for a couple weeks to be a medical depression, but it's so much easier to package the full continuum into a single term. Anyway, what a great test of my Stoicism!
Stoicism demands that I have a clear understanding of what I control and what I do not. I've mentioned before that Stoics consider even my own body as outside my complete control. That principle isn't very hard to apply to aches in my joints, but things get murkier when it comes to my emotional states. Where do emotions fall on the control spectrum? After all, they're so closely related to the all important stoic will. Epictetus listed the things in my control as: opinion, pursuit, desire, and aversion. There's definitely an emotional component to such terms as pursuit, desire, and aversion. So how should I treat my emotional state during depression?

My emotions are *indifferent* when they are not coupled with my opinions. This is completely my own thought, I can't back it up with Stoic quotes and such (maybe I'll be able to in the future). Still, look at this Aurelius quote: *Today I have got out of all trouble, or rather I have cast out all trouble, for it was not outside, but within and* **in my opinions.** Opinions come up a lot in Stoicism. This makes sense, opinions are formed by all the aspects of our mind that Stoics find important, like the will and reason. So the question becomes, where do my emotions meet my opinions?

I believe that my depression arrives prior to my negative thoughts. By which I mean, my brain becomes chemically imbalanced and it makes happy thoughts *oh so hard* to generate while stressful thoughts flow like water on a downhill slope. As such, my emotional state would be indifferent, neither virtue nor vice. My emotions are simply part of the environment I find myself in. On the other hand, if I couple my emotions with my opinions, I am moved towards desire or aversion. In that case, my emotions become part of a process that is either virtuous or not.

If this is a workable concept in Stoicism, then treating my depression as an indifferent should led to tranquility. I'm happy to report it did. Not instantly, but my depression lasted days, not weeks. It worked like this: One day I wake up and basically feel muted. The world is sepia, with all the emotional color drained out of it. Half a day later, I start the standard process of building my thoughts on a scaffolding of depressed emotions, leading to an even darker place. Thankfully, I have developed a habit of reviewing Stoic quotes and the like. I begin questioning the nature of my depression. I decide that my emotional state is outside my control. As such, I refuse to predicate my approach to the world on my present emotional state. I fulfill all my duties, listen to and accept good advice from my wife, surround myself with good friends, and basically continue life without paying attention to my dull internal world. Within 48-hours, my chemical imbalance corrects itself. Which is record time. Thanks, Stoicism!

9

When People Are Obstacles

Good Fortune: Episode Seven

It never ceases to amaze me: we all love ourselves more than other people, but care more about their opinion than our own.
(*Meditations* 12:4)

People can be a pain. It's not just me, right? People are rude, they back stab, they put their own projects above yours even when you're meant to be on the same team. I'm not a misanthrope (no Stoic should be) but I definitely laughed at a recent tweet from Existential Comics; "I feel like humanity really went wrong when we first decided to speak to each other. Nothing good has come from it."

Hi, I'm Matt Van Natta and this is Good Fortune. Today's questions:

- What do I do when people are the obstacles?
- How can I remain my best self when everyone else is being their worst self?
- When does a Stoic call it quits?

Alright, let's get started...

What do I do when people are the obstacles?

Sometimes the biggest challenges in life have first names. You might be a pleasant, happy go lucky, turn the other cheek sort of person, but that's no guarantee that someone won't decide you're in their way.

How are we supposed to handle these situations. Tit for tat and an eye for an eye? Allow them to roll right over us? Some middle ground between those extremes? Well, we're here to talk about Stoicism, so you can bet that before we wrestle with our adversary we must first get our own perspective in order.

Here's another thought from Emperor Aurelius from Book 7, Chapter 26;

> When people injure you, ask yourself what good or harm they thought would come of it. If you understand that, you'll feel sympathy rather than outrage or anger. Your sense of good and evil may be the same as theirs, in which case you have to excuse them. Or your sense of good and evil may differ from theirs. In which case they're misguided and deserve your compassion. Is that so hard?

Actually, yes Aurelius, it can be really hard. However, it's a noble goal to strive for. But before we do, a caveat. Never allow Stoicism to be a 'blame the victim' philosophy. Callousness, cruelty, and the like are wrong. Truly. Stoicism does not diminish that, nor does it absolve others of whatever injustices they perpetrate. What we're recognizing is that, unfortunately, we can't change what has happened, we can only choose how to respond. The mental realignment that Marcus Aurelius recommends, this attempt to develop sympathy and compassion for others, is meant to fuel our own virtuous actions. Instead of responding in kind, we respond Stoically, with the welfare of all involved in mind.

In the next section, I'll talk more in depth about developing sympathy and compassion. But for now, let's stick with simply accepting the situation we're in. Here's another Aurelius based technique (everything this episode is coming out of the *Meditations*, the Emperor's life at court obviously meant working with a lot of devious, scheming individuals and he had a lot to say about it);

> In the ring, our opponents can gouge us with their nails or butt us with their heads and leave a bruise, but we don't denounce them for it or get upset with them or regard them from then on as violent types. We just keep an eye on them

after that. Not out of hatred or suspicion, just keeping a friendly distance.

We need to do that in other areas. We need to excuse what our sparring partners do, and just keep our distance – without suspicion or hatred.

If you've listened to Episode Two you may remember Aurelius' morning meditation, his reminder to himself that when going about his day, it's inevitable that some people will be obstacles. This wrestling analogy is similar. There are rules in wrestling, you're not supposed to get gouged, headbutted, and the like. But sports are messy. Sometimes things go wrong. Taking part in a sport means accepting that danger. We should approach life the same way. Sometimes we're scratched up by others because we're in the wrong place at the wrong time. Our co-worker might be a jerk just because she needs to get her blood sugar up! Who knows? At times it's best to not take it personal. Still, we keep an eye on them and a friendly distance. The benefit of the doubt doesn't mean we have to keep ourselves in a precarious situation.

Now, I've been assuming that we're in the right in all these situations. One more line from *Meditations* before we move on. Book 10, Chapter 37; "Learn to ask of all actions, 'Why are they doing that?' Starting with your own."

How can I remain my best self when everyone else is being their worst self?
Now it's time to work on our ability to feel sympathy and compassion for our adversaries. We begin by asking of every action a person does, "Why are they doing that?" The key is to not answer the question with, "because they're a jerk," or "because they are evil!" In Stoic thought all people are always looking to do good (as they understand it), because they want the best for themselves. So we can also ask, "what good did they think would come from this?" If I'm in customer service and a customer I've never met decides to berate me about store policy, why? What does she think the outcome is going to be? Does she believe yelling is the simplest way to get to speak to a manager? Does she think it gives her greater power in the situation? Is her anger just covering the frustration and disappointment of a horrible day?

Any of those reasons may be unreasonable to you, but her actions are reasonable considering her personal subjective beliefs about the world. Understanding this can give you at least three benefits. One, as Aurelius said, "When people injure you, ask yourself what good or harm they thought would come of it. If you understand that, you'll feel sympathy rather than outrage or anger." However, even if you can't raise up any sympathy in yourself, understanding their reasoning can lead to benefit two, a better chance of diffusing the situation. Because if you understand what they really want, if you can step out of yourself and into their mind for a moment, you can possibly provide what they need. Three, you can demystify their social status.

Alright, that's a weird way to say what I'm thinking. In *Meditations* Book 9, Chapter 27, the first lines say,

"When you face someone's insults, hatred or whatever…look at his soul. Get inside him. Look at what sort of person he is. You'll find you don't need to strain to impress him…"

Emperor Aurelius has notes throughout his journal that remind him of the same thing, that if look at who your adversaries really are you won't bend over backwards to impress them. And he was the Emperor! Who was he trying to impress? Well, I opened with this quote, "It never ceases to amaze me: we all love ourselves more than other people, but care more about their opinion than our own." People at all levels of status fall into this need to impress others, to endear ourselves to others. Sometimes we have to shed that burden before we can act well. Yes, the person who's yelling at me right now is a Senator, but I'm not here to endear myself to the powerful, I'm here to do right the best I know how. Of course, while we're not "straining to impress people" we are still treating them with humanity. Chapter 27 continues, "But you do have to wish him well. He is your closest relative. The gods assist him, just as they do you…" So we're not taking them down a peg so that we can feel superior. We're just reminding ourselves that our job is to do our best, not necessarily to make others happy.

I'm going to end this section with an avalanche of quotes:

"The tranquility that comes when you stop caring what they say. Or think, or do. Only what you do. (Is it fair? Is it the right thing to do?)" (4:18)

and

"So other people hurt me? That's their problem. What is done to me is ordained by nature, what I do by my own." (5:25)

also

"If an action or utterance is appropriate, then it's appropriate for you. Don't be put off by other people's comments and criticism. If it's right to say or do it, then it's the right thing to do or say.

The others obey their own lead, follow their own impulses. Don't be distracted. Keep walking. Follow your own nature, and follow Nature–along the road they share." (5:3)

finally

"Someone despises me. That's their problem.

Mine: Not to say or do anything despicable.

Someone hates me. Their problem.

Mine: To be patient and cheerful with everyone, including them. Ready to show them their mistake. Not spitefully, or to show off my own self-control, but in an honest, upright way...That's what we should be like inside, and never let the gods catch us feeling anger or resentment.

As long as you do what's proper to your nature, and accept what the world's nature has in store–as long as you work for other's good, by any and all means–what is there that can harm you?" (11:13)

When does a Stoic call it quits?

Here's *Meditations* Book 6, Chapter 50:

> Do your best to convince them. But act on your own, if justice requires it. If met with force, fall back on acceptance and peacability. Use the setback to practice other virtues. Remember that our efforts are subject to circumstances, you weren't aiming to do the impossible.
>
> –Aiming to do what then?
>
> To try. And you succeeded. What you set out to do is accomplished.

There's a lot to unpack here. But to understand Aurelius' position. we need to talk about the Stoic **Reserve Clause**.

I will get this podcast out on time, God willing. You've heard people say god willing before, right? Maybe you say it? To some people it has meaning, to others it may just be a cultural habit, like saying bless you after a person sneezes. For the ancient Stoics, god willing, or more specifically, Zeus willing, was an important philosophical exercise. Oh, and for anyone who who may not want to invoke God/Zeus or the like, here are two other possibilities to express a similar sentiment. "Fate permitting, I will get this podcast out on time. or simply, "I will get this podcast out on time, if nothing prevents me."

OK. We've talked before about what is in our control. The Reserve Clause is a means of applying the control/not in our control dichotomy to our plans in life. Donald Robertson, in his book, *The Philosophy of Cognitive Behavioural Therapy*, says that,

> The Stoic...makes a point of qualifying the expression of every intention, by introducing a distinction between his will and external factors beyond his control. The Sage thereby holds two complementary propositions in mind simultaneously, *viz.*,
> 1. I will do my very best to succeed.
> 2. While simultaneously accepting that the ultimate outcome is beyond my direct control.

Think of archery; the original Stoics often did. An archer can choose equipment, draw back properly, aim well, and release, but the moment that arrow is off the bow string, the archer has no control. A gust of wind could mean missing the target. A strong wind could mean the target falls over! The archer does their best to maximize the chance that the arrow hits the target, but they can't control the outcome. And similarly, Aurelius asks himself to, "remember that our efforts are subject to circumstances, you weren't aiming to do the impossible. -Aiming to do what then? To try. And you succeeded. What you set out to do is accomplished." Stoics take the best action we can with the information we have. Sometimes we don't hit the mark, our best case scenario doesn't materialize. No matter, we'll keep doing good in the situation that is at hand. We, "use the setback to practice other virtues."

So when does a Stoic call it quits? In one sense, never. We live our lives aiming to take virtuous actions, and we never run out of opportunities to do this. If we think and act well, we are always succeeding. But when do we end a project in life, decide a particular outcome isn't going to happen, and move on? Well, if the only way to make something happen would require us to be unjust, foolish, cowardly, or greedy, we should abandon that project. Otherwise, feel free to keep going until wisdom tells you it's time to do something new. We're all fortunate to have an infinite quiver of arrows with which we can attempt to hit the mark.

10

How Stoics Treat Jerks

People. What a bunch of bastards!
(*The IT Crowd*)

Stoics love people, even the bastards. The heart of our philosophy is love for humankind. The virtue that we seek to cultivate can only be properly expressed in relationship to our human family. We agree with Marcus Aurelius who reminded himself that, "your only joy, and your only rest, is to pass from one action performed in the service of the human community to another action performed in the service of the human community." Stoicism is often framed as a lonely discipline, encouraging men to stand apart from the crowd, but that is so far from the truth. Stoic wisdom is meant to enhance the humanity of those who practice it. We are participating with the crowd. We may not act as the crowd would expect or demand, but we always seek to act with our neighbor's best interest at heart. That said, how are Stoics to respond when faced with disagreeable people?

> It is within a man's power to love even those who sin against him. This becomes possible when you realize that they are your brothers, that they wrong you unintentionally or out of ignorance, that in a little while you and they will be dead, and above all, that they have not really hurt you so long as you have not sullied your conscience or damaged your inner self by responding in kind.
> (*Meditations* 7:22)

Marcus Aurelius spent a lot of time preparing himself to interact with awful people. The Emperor did not find his court to be filled with the most uplifting sorts of citizens. So in many of his meditations he would dwell on the formula found in the quote above;

- humans are all family
- no one intentionally makes an error in judgement
- life is short
- a Stoic **can not** be morally hurt by others; Stoics can only harm themselves through a vicious response

I've addressed the human family before, so I won't elaborate here. It is worth taking a moment to think about the second point; the Stoic principle that no one means to do wrong. Stoicism considers all immorality to be a form of ignorance. It works something like this;

- only reasoned choices are moral
- all people choose actions that they believe are best for themselves in the moment
- 'evil' choices are never the true best choices
- therefore, a person who does wrong is ignorant of the better way

This way of thinking should have a huge impact on how a Stoic treats disagreeable people. If we truly believe that the people who wrong us are simply ignorant, what is the appropriate response? Epictetus addresses this issue in chapter 42 of the *Enchiridion*:

> When any person harms you, or speaks badly of you, remember that he acts or speaks from a supposition of its being his duty. Now, it is not possible that he should follow what appears right to you, but what appears so to himself. Therefore, if he judges from a wrong appearance, he is the person hurt, since he too is the person deceived. For if anyone should suppose a true proposition to be false, the proposition is not hurt, but he who is deceived about it. *Setting out, then, from these principles, you will meekly bear a person who reviles you, for you will say upon every occasion, 'It seemed so to him.'*

"It seemed so to him." This is a position of sympathy. In Stoicism, ignorance is not reviled, it is simply corrected. Epictetus, like Aurelius, clams that the person who is hurt by immorality is the person who performs it. The Stoic is left unscathed, assuming he reacts appropriately. One last Aurelius quote, "People exist for the sake of one another. Teach them then, or bear with them." I used this quote in the article I linked to earlier. In that post I viewed *bear with them* as a call for something like patience. I think I was mistaken. The more I dwell on the Stoic insistence that we truly love others, the more it sounds like a call to shoulder their burdens. Most daily insults do not happen during teachable moments but they do always arrive with the opportunity to enact virtue. In doing so, we not only stay true to ourselves, we bring good into the world.

Stoics are meant to see the common humanity of everyone we meet. With that kinship in mind, we bear up under the weight of unjust actions and, if possible, point out a better way. If we truly embrace the Stoic perspective, this isn't difficult. Our point of view contains no fuel that could feed indignation. We're left free to act with compassion, and through compassion we show the strength of our philosophy.

11

Nine Ways to Stop Being Upset by Others

> **Commit these nine observations to memory**; accept them as gifts from the Muses; and while you still have life, begin to live…
> (*Meditations* 11:18)

I keep track of my thoughts about Stoicism in a notebook that I try to keep near me. Most of its pages are incoherent; containing scattered musings from recent readings or reminders to revisit some chapter or other when I get the chance. From time to time, however, a Stoic author lays out an idea in such a succinct manner that the notes I create from it are practical. Book 11, Chapter 18 of Aurelius' *Meditations* is just such a usable bit of writing.

These four questions and five reminders are a certain means of regaining a Stoic mindset if we are set off balance by the day's social interactions. Of course, in order for them to be effective, we need a clear understanding of the worldview that informs the exercise.

- What is my relationship to others?

Marcus Aurelius' short answer is, "we are made for each other." The Stoic view is that our highest purpose is fulfilled by serving others. We should seek to do right by everyone we meet, even if they are not returning the favor.

- What sort of person is upsetting me?

Evaluate the person you're dealing with. Aurelius breaks this down into sub-questions: What actions do their opinions compel them to perform and to what extent are their actions motivated by pride? Stoics never expect people with bad information to make good decisions.

- Are they right?!

Check yourself. You could be the one that's in the wrong. Never forget that you are fallible.

- Do I understand the context?

Aurelius reminds us that, "Many things are done for reasons that are not apparent. A man must know a great deal before condemning another person's behavior." Looking back to the question "are they right," the Stoic default position is, "I don't know." It's difficult enough to keep ourselves on a consistent path of virtue, why waste time guessing where someone else is at?

- I also make mistakes.

If we expect any grace from others when we stumble, shouldn't we be willing to give the same to them?

- Life is too short.

"Think…how soon you and your vexations will be laid in the grave." Aurelius didn't want to spend his time angry and impatient when he could, instead, pursue happiness. It's sound advice.

- I am actually disturbing myself.

Stoics hold ourselves responsible for our emotions. As Epictetus put it, "it is not circumstances themselves that trouble people, but their judgement about those circumstances." It's important to realize that we can't control how others act, but we can choose how we will respond. Aurelius reminds himself that, "it isn't what others do that troubles you. That is on their own consciences. You are bothered by your opinions of what they do. Rid yourself of those opinions and stop assuming the worst – then your troubles will go away. How do you get rid of your opinions? By reminding yourself that you aren't disgraced by what others do."

- I am choosing to prolong my suffering.

"Our rage and lamentations do us more harm than whatever caused our anger and grief in the first place." Again Aurelius lays bare the ridiculousness of fuming about another person's actions.

- A good disposition is invincible.

"What can the most insolent man do if you remain relentlessly kind and, given the opportunity, counsel him calmly and gently even while he's trying to harm you?" I sort of love the term "relentlessly kind." If we succeed at keeping a Stoic mindset during every social interaction, then we will genuinely value each and every person we meet. This would have to be unnerving! I'm picturing a salesperson who is speaking nicely but seems to have spite behind their eyes. However, Aurelius isn't counseling a faux friendliness. In fact, he continues, "Let their be nothing ironic or scolding in your tone, but speak with true affection and with no residue of resentment in your heart. Don't lecture him. Don't embarrass him in front of others. But address him privately even if others are present.

We're not going to run out of situations that make these points useful. Emperor Aurelius advised himself to memorize them. You may want to as well. Or, like me, you might choose to carry a reminder with you. I know that when I turn to the nine points of *Meditations* 11:18, I find it impossible to continue stoking the anger that's in me. I'm reminded of the practical outcomes that are expected from a lived Stoic philosophy. I realize that if I truly believe that all people have value and that we are meant to work together, I can not act against that truth and consider myself reasonable. I suspect that taking a page from Aurelius will work just as well for you.

12

Fighting Non-Stoic Thoughts
Infernal Monologue

I've had a lot of fights where I was the only participant. Thankfully, they've all happened in my head and not in a scene out of Fight Club. The animosity of these intense moments is rarely directed at myself. Whichever poor soul I'm dwelling on isn't actually present, I've conjured him up with my overactive imagination. Sometimes I'm steeped in a moment where I felt slighted. Other times I'm envisioning future disagreements that I imagine are heading towards me. Sometimes I'm simply shadowboxing, beating up some straw-man standing in for a viewpoint I find hard to tolerate. Fantasizing of this type is anti-Stoic. It's the willful practice of negative emotions and misanthropic thoughts! It's as far afield as one can get from the present-focused attention that Stoicism demands. So what to do?

> Stop fantasizing! Cut the strings of desire that keep you dancing like a puppet. Draw a circle around the present moment. Recognize what is happening either to you or to someone else. Dissect everything into its causal and material elements. Ponder your final hour. Leave the wrong with the person who did it.
> (*Meditations* 7:29)

Aurelius' first line has also been translated, "wipe out the imagination," but I believe "fantasizing" better captures his meaning. The Emperor doesn't want to waste his life working himself up over the unreal. To combat his wandering thoughts, he reminds himself of five stoic mental practices:

- Attend to the present moment
- Focus on what affects people here and now
- Break things down until they are understandable and manageable
- Remember that life is short
- "Leave the wrong with the person who did it."

My internal monologue, like Aurelius', is often far removed from the here and now. In contrast, the stoic mind is rooted in the present, because the present moment is the only time in which a Stoic can exercise control. Seneca put it this way, "These two things must be cut away: fear of the future, and the memory of past sufferings. The latter no longer concern me, and the future does not concern me yet." We regain our footing by attending to what is happening now.

When Stoics decide what to do in the present moment, our thoughts should be concerned with the people we can help. As Aurelius reminds himself in Chapter 9 of his *Meditations*, "Passivity with regard to the events brought about by an exterior cause. Justice in the actions brought about by the cause that is within you. In other words, let your impulse to act and your action have as their goal the service of the human community, because that, for you, is in conformity with your nature." Chances are, if I were to pay attention to what's happening to the people around me, I'd find something better to do than daydream.

The Emperor's self-admonition to, "dissect everything into its causal and material elements," is a bit more esoteric. Donald Robertson, in his book *Stoicism and the Art of Happiness*, explains it like this:

> The Stoic strategy of seeing the present moment in isolation…appears to be closely related to another technique…called 'physical definition'. This involves cultivating the calm detachment of a natural philosopher or scientist. We are to practice describing an object or event purely in terms of its objective qualities, stripped of any emotive rhetoric or value judgments, to arrive at an

'objective representation' (*phantasia kataléptiké*)... However, especially in the writings of Marcus Aurelius, this may also involve a kind of 'method of division', in which the event becomes broken down through analysis, calmly dissected into its individual components or aspects.

By breaking things down into smaller parts, Aurelius seeks to demystify the happenings in life. For instance, to get past lust he memorably describes sex as, "friction of the genitals with the excretion of mucus in spasms." Now that's a mood killer. Speaking of killer, on to our impending doom!

"Ponder your final hour," is a Stoic version of YOLO. Life is short. If we want life to have meaning, we should build that meaning in the here and now, not in our imaginations. Unfortunately death is a taboo subject in western society so it would take too long to make a case for the positive aspects of dwelling on mortality. However, check out HereIsToday.com, if you want to meditate on how the lifespan of the universe makes us all look like mayflies. I know that if I really took the shortness of life to heart, I'd stop wasting thoughts on some guy that cut me off an hour ago.

Marcus Aurelius' final advice to himself is, "leave the wrong with the person who did it." Why burden ourselves with someone else's moral failings? Don't we have enough of our own problems to worry about? Of course, this doesn't mean we allow people to do evil things. Stoic actions are for the good of humankind, after all. But we should not burn with indignation at another person's actions. Instead, we should make certain that our own thoughts and actions are good, since that's all that we truly control.

Each of these five techniques rely on a core stoic skill, the ability to pay attention. Stoicism can only be practiced with an attentive mind.

> Attention is the fundamental Stoic spiritual attitude. It is a continuous vigilance and presence of mind, self-consciousness which never sleeps, and a constant tension of the spirit. Thanks to this attitude, the philosopher is fully aware of what he does at each instant, and he wills his actions fully.

(Pierre Hadot)

There's no such thing as unconscious Stoicism. Attention is fundamental. When my mind is wandering, I'm losing out. I'm denying myself the pleasure of living a life of impact and meaning. In those moments I am not Stoic. Thankfully, a quick reminder of what *is* Stoic, and the will to put that into practice is all it takes to get back on the path. It's simple, but strenuous. Hadot's, "constant tension of the spirit," requires dedication. Thankfully, the long gone Stoics of the past left me a few Cliff Notes to help out along the way. I hope your internal monologue is less infernal than mine, but if not, I hope these techniques are as helpful to you as they are to me.

13

The Blame Game

On Stoic Progress

> It is not circumstances themselves that trouble people, but their judgments about those circumstances. For example, death is nothing terrible, for if it were, it would have appeared so to Socrates; but having the opinion that death is terrible, this is what is terrible. Therefore, whenever we are hindered or troubled or distressed, let us not blame others, but ourselves, that is, our own judgments. **The uneducated person blames others for their failures; those who have just begun to be instructed blame themselves; those whose learning is complete blame neither others nor themselves.**
>
> (*Enchiridion* 5)

Measuring progress in a lived philosophy isn't necessarily simple. Stoicism is meant to establish a "good flow of life" in its adherents. For instance, a person who is living well will be calm in the face of adversity, if not joyful. They will also use their skills to benefit their community, and seek to expand the very idea of community as wide as possible. The impact of lived Stoicism should be apparent to all but, because of its holistic nature, can sometimes be difficult to point out, even to ourselves. We are often more comfortable with a simple checklist.

Unfortunately, when something can be itemized, it's often not very useful as a measure of progress. It is far too easy to turn to false indicators (number of books read, quotes memorized, or arguments won) as a gauge of success. Even a positive indicator can be misleading. I may maintain a calm demeanor all day, not because I stoically accept the world *warts and all*, but because I wasn't faced with any potential obstacles to my tranquility. Thankfully, every once in a while an ancient Stoic points to an indicator that is hard to fake.

> The uneducated person blames others for their failures; those who have just begun to be instructed blame themselves; those whose learning is complete blame neither others nor themselves.

Epictetus says that Stoics blame themselves for moral failures. That's pretty cut and dried. As long as I am honest with myself, I can review my weak moments and see who or what I blamed. Did I claim that, "the traffic made me angry"? Was my co-worker, "so frustrating"? If so, I wasn't approaching those events as a Stoic. If I instead told myself, "I shouldn't have become angry today in traffic," or,"why did I decide to frustrate myself just because Jake can't do his job," then I messed up in the moment, but I recovered. Taking the blame is, in itself, a sign of progress. If I go a step further and avoid any anger and frustration in the first place, all the better! By the way, Stoics *don't* blame themselves for the events that are happening to them. Traffic isn't my fault, after all. We *do*, however, accept control over our reaction to life. Our reactions, based in our judgment of the situation, are firmly in the moral sphere.

So if you're trying to live the Stoic life, where are you placing blame? Epictetus says it's all on you. If you're like me, you might prefer to skip the blame game and move on to living blamelessly, but let's face it, that's not going to happen. *It is not circumstances themselves that trouble people, but their judgments about those circumstances.* That is a fundamental truth of our philosophy. It takes daily work to internalize it. If we don't, we won't have a good flow of life, and there will be no one to blame but ourselves.

14

Citizen of the World

> Let us take hold of the fact that there are two communities — the one, which is great and truly common, embracing gods and humans, in which we look neither to this corner nor to that, but measure the boundaries of our citizenship by the sun; the other, the one to which we have been assigned by the accident of our birth.
> (Seneca)

The ancient Stoics were one of the first Western philosophies to advocate cosmopolitanism, the idea that we are citizens of the world. They insisted that rational beings are bonded through our similar needs and goals and, therefore, we should live for the well being of all. Stoicism is meant to expand our affection for one another until there is no one who is "other." Epictetus states in *Discourses* 2.10 that a Stoic will, "hold nothing as profitable to himself and deliberate about nothing as if he were detached from the community, but act as the hand or foot would do, if they had reason and understood the constitution of nature, for they would never put themselves in motion nor desire anything, otherwise than with reference to the whole." The Stoic perspective is a communal and universal one. Many of our exercises, e.g. The View From Above, serve to bake that all encompassing worldview into our mind. It is, therefore, the duty of every Stoic to reject the constant othering that society perpetuates and instead accept all people as they are.

When we consider ourselves "right," we consider ourselves better. At least, that's what online conversations about opposing political parties, religious views, and the like seem to suggest. Did you know that everyone else is an idiot at best, evil at worst? Twitter and Facebook sure do. We live in a world that comes together through exclusion. Stoics are not meant to think that way. We should not believe ourselves better, we should believe ourselves blessed.

Actually, I'd prefer to call myself fortunate, but blessed made for decent alliteration. I am fortunate to be practicing a philosophy that brings such contentment. Not everyone has the same foundation to stand on. Marcus Aurelius told himself to, "begin each day by telling yourself: Today I will be meeting with interference, ingratitude, insolence, disloyalty, ill-will, and selfishness – all of this due to the offenders' ignorance of what is good and what is evil." Stoics believe wrong action comes from ignorance of a better way. Ignorance is unfortunate, and sometimes tragic, but it's not worth disparaging those who are ignorant. In fact, Epictetus considered forbearance of others intimately linked to Stoicism's central tenets.

> Let me state once again the basic rule of our philosophy: the greatest harm a person can suffer is the loss of his most valuable possession, his Reason. The harm he creates for himself is not transferred to others. Therefore, there is no reason for others to become angry because a person commits a crime against himself.
> (*Discourses* 1.18.1-10)

I address this because there is a tendency among armchair philosophers to build up their "wisdom" by disparaging others. Practicing Stoics should be outside of that conversation. Aurelius said, "People exist for the sake of one another. Teach them then, or bear with them." Bear with them. It isn't even a high calling. We're not being asked to hold a Free Hugs sign. We're being asked to live as Stoics.

The ideals of Stoicism are perfectly suited for the world in which we're living: they've just been sadly under utilized since 300 BCE. Stoic cosmopolitanism demands more than lip service. Stoics engage with the world. Our philosophy was born in the public square, and it's meant to stay there. That engagement has to stem from virtue. We're not meant to be protesters simply waving signs in people's faces to tell them they're wrong. We're meant to be building something true and lasting; adding to the well being of our local and global community. Find contentment in wisdom itself, not in the tangential belief that Stoicism means you're on the right side. Bear this life as a Stoic.

15

The Stoic Love of Community

Did you know that the Stoic view of humanity is one of love, compassion, and concern? It is. However, if you missed this fact, I wouldn't be surprised. The common conception of the 'stoic' individual doesn't immediately bring to mind an enthusiastic and engaged community member. Even as Stoicism has surged in popularity, much of the conversation has remained focused on the philosophy's psychological tool kit without going on to address the wider Stoic view of the world. This is unfortunate. Stoic psychology is a powerful system that can build mindfulness and resilience into its practitioners. Such inner strength is helpful for everyone, but it becomes admirable when applied to the real problems of the world. One of my favorite descriptions of Stoicism well-lived comes from Seneca. He writes,

> No school has more goodness and gentleness; none has more love for human beings, nor more attention to the common good. The goal which it assigns to us is to be useful, to help others, and to take care, not only of ourselves, but of everyone in general and of each one in particular
> (*On Clemency* 3.3)

What a vibrant description! The philosophy to which Seneca had devoted himself did not encourage detachment. The Stoicism he had learned and lived was deeply engaged with world. It was, and continues to be, a philosophy of community. Its goal is to bring the best out of Stoics so they, in turn, can give their best to the people around them. These community-embracing Stoics are not the aloof men and women of popular conception. They are the friends, neighbors, and citizens who take up the hard work of life because they are not concerned with the obstacles in their way.

As an example of this community focus, let's look at the Stoic concept of *oikeiôsis*. A lot of meaning is packed into that odd word which makes it difficult to translate, but words like *affinity*, *affiliation*, and *endearment* cover many of its facets. Stoicism claims that humans have a natural affinity for one another. This natural affection begins as love of the self, but quickly grows to encompass our caregivers and close family. In the Stoic view, the wise will work to expand this endearment until it covers each and every person. The clearest example of this is given by Hierocles, a Stoic contemporary of Marcus Aurelius. Hierocles spoke of a series of expanding circles. The first circle is our individual self, the next is our family, then our local community, our nation, and lastly the whole of humanity. As we grow our Stoic *oikeiôsis*, we are required to bring people from the outer circles into nearer ones. We challenge our perception of humankind until we can say that all people are our sisters and brothers. The expected outcome is that all our actions will consider their needs of others as equal to our own.

Stoicism interacts with the outmost circle, the whole of humankind, through the lens of cosmopolitanism. The ancient Stoics referred to themselves as citizens of the world. To them, all the barriers to human cooperation whether political, economic, or social were irrational constructs. At our human best, we are capable of working with anyone because, as Marcus Aurelius reminds himself, "…we were born into this world to work together like the feet, hands, eyelids, or upper and lower rows of teeth" (*Meditations* 2.1). This body-focused imagery is found throughout Stoic teaching. Humans are treated as part of a single organism, wherein our individual selves are best served by taking into account everyone's needs. The teacher Epictetus actually combines the concept of citizenship with this body imagery:

> What then does the character of a citizen promise? To hold nothing as profitable to himself; to deliberate about nothing as if we were detached from the community, but

to act as the hand or foot would do, if they had reason and
understood the constitution of nature, for they would never
put themselves in motion nor desire anything, otherwise
than with reference to the whole

(*Discourses* 2.10)

This outlook explains why so many ancient Stoics were bold political animals. Did they separate events into what they could and could not control? Yes. Did they consider the actions of others and the happenings of life as indifferent to their purpose? Again, yes. How did they use the freedom they found through disregarding the external obstacles of life? Stoic freedom was fuel for brave actions taken in the name of what was just.

Marcus Aurelius said to, "let your impulse to act and your action have as their goal the service of the human community, because that, for you, is in conformity with your nature" (*Meditations* 9.31). What does it mean for us, as modern Stoics, to serve the human community? I don't believe there is any one clear answer. The world is complex, and we all inhabit unique spaces and have individual strengths and shortcomings. Some of us may have the wherewithal to engage in higher level politics. Some of us may be interested in making our neighborhood school a better place. Personally, I try to serve my community during disasters large and small through the Red Cross. I'm guessing that all of us are aware of inequities and imperfections worth addressing in our communities. As Stoics, we have the fortitude to act courageously on behalf of others. We should use that strength.

Of course, modern politics seems to be built on division and strife. Even something as simple as improving a local park is guaranteed to rile up passions and conflict. How are we supposed to go out and fight for justice while remaining our serene stoic selves? By practicing Stoicism! In particular, we can use the Stoic reserve clause to maintain our tranquility during long term projects. The reserve clause is the Stoic habit of saying that we will do this or that, "fate permitting." It's a constant reminder that our actions are up to us, but the outcomes are outside of our control. As Seneca says, "In short, the wise man looks to the purpose of all actions, not their consequences; beginnings are in our power but Fortune judges the outcome, and I do not grant her a verdict upon me" (*Letters* 14). This is an outlook that encourages Stoics to think big. Does something in your neighborhood need to change? Go change it. Will you succeed? Who knows? Do your best work and be satisfied in doing it. 'Don't wait for Plato's Republic! Rather, be content if one tiny thing makes some progress, and reflect on the fact that what results from this tiny thing is no tiny thing at all!' (*Meditations* 9.29).

Stoicism is community focused. Stoic mental practices were developed to free us to thrive in the face of the world as it is. The freedom we gain, in turn, allows us to act with conviction. We may not all change the world, but we can each find our one tiny thing. Many people, doing many tiny things, can add up to something big. Even if it doesn't, at least we were able to practice our Stoicism. That in itself is worth doing.

16

When We Stumble

Good Fortune: Episode Eight

Are you a Stoic Sage yet? Hahaha…I'm kidding, of course. You're not. I'm not. No one is. We're loaded with all the inconsistencies that make us human. We're petty, needy, dismissive, cruel, thoughtless, perhaps all these things within a single hour! So how do we start over? How do we reset, knowing that we were so embarrassingly wrong a minute ago, or yesterday, or for entire years of our life? How do we press on knowing we'll probably screw up again tomorrow? What do we do when we stumble?

Hi, I'm Matt Van Natta and this is Good Fortune. Today's questions:

- How am I supposed to react when I screw up?
- How can I stop blaming myself (should I stop blaming myself?) when the fact is I really did do something wrong?
- And finally, what exercise can get me back into my Stoic practice?

Alright, let's get started…

How am I supposed to react when I screw up?

Let's begin with a mindset to aim towards. Here's the beginning of *Meditations* 5:9:

> Not to feel exasperated, or defeated, or despondent because your days aren't packed with wise and moral actions. But

to get back up when you fail, to celebrate behaving like a human –however imperfectly– and fully embrace the pursuit you've embarked on.

That sounds healthy, right? Pick yourself up, dust off, and get going again. Yet I've been in places where my shame cuts deep. Where I can't forsee others ever forgiving me and I don't really think I deserve to forgive myself. What then?

If you are living out Stoicism, however imperfectly, you are a *prokopton*. Prokopton is a Greek word that's applied to Stoic students, though prokopton does not mean 'student.' It means, a 'person who is progressing.' So we are progressors pursuing moral progress; which is a very difficult task. We're likely to lose ground from time to time, take a step forward and then two back. This is natural, unfortunate, but natural. Of course, bad fortune born nobly is good fortune, so with that in mind, we have to begin viewing our failings as lessons and use what we learn about ourselves to readjust and carry on.

In the *Discourses* Book 3, Chapter 25, lines 1-4, Epictetus has this to say about our personal failures:

> Of the things that you initially proposed for yourself, consider which you have achieved and which you haven't, and how it gives you joy to recall some of them and pain to recall others, and, if possible, try to recover even those that have slipped from your grasp. For those who are engaged in the greatest of contests shouldn't flinch, but must be prepared also to take blows. For the contest that lies in front of us is not in wrestling or the pancration, in which, whether or not one meets with success, it is possible for one to be of the highest worth or of little, and by Zeus, to be most happy or most miserable; no, this is a contest for good fortune and happiness itself. What follows, then? In this contest, even if we should falter for a while, no one can prevent us from resuming the fight, nor is it necessary to wait another four years for the next Olympic Games to come around, but as soon as one has recovered and regained one's strength, and can muster the same zeal as before, one

can enter the fight; and if one should fail again, one can enter once again, and if one should carry off the victory one fine day, it will be as if one had never given in.

We are in a contest for the best things, the things that will allow us to flourish. And this is a contest that we can reenter whenever we're ready. Best yet, if we finally win, our past record gets wiped away. Meaning that true contentment banishes the ghosts of past failures. Not because we pretend we didn't harm others but because we can look the facts in the eyes and simply choose to do better. It's the hurting person, the one that can't overcome past mistakes who hides from the truth of who they've been and therefore continues to make the same mistakes. The flourishing individual is able to take up the hard work of facing others, acknowledge our mistakes, and repair the damage if possible. We need to follow Epictetus' advice, recover, regain our strength, muster our zeal, and begin again.

How can I stop blaming myself (should I stop blaming myself) when the fact is I really did do something wrong?

Before we learn to stop blaming ourselves, let's recall why Stoics don't blame others. Here's the end of Chapter 5 of the *Enchiridion*:

> ...whenever we are hindered or troubled or distressed, let us never blame others, but ourselves, that is, our own judgments. The uneducated person blames others for their failures; those who have just begun to be instructed blame themselves; those whose learning is complete blame neither others nor themselves.

It's not that other people don't do wrong, it's that they can't make us do wrong. It's our own actions that we control, so that's where we place our energy. The devil did not make me do it, I failed myself. So Epictetus says the uneducated blame others, we progressors blame ourselves, but the ones who really get it blame neither themselves nor others. What does he mean by that?

Some have interpreted Epictetus' final remark to be speaking of the perfect Stoic Sage, a mythic figure who never is at fault and therefore can not be blamed. I would like to propose a different and, I believe, more practical reading. In my view the still imperfect, but fully educated Stoic has realized and internalized that the same Stoic understanding which allows us to accept and pity the errors of other people can also and should also be applied to ourselves.

In Stoicism, moral failings are due to ignorance of a better way to act. All people honestly strive for what is expedient for them and if they choose wrongly, it's because they were ignorant of the better solution. To back this up we can again look to Epictetus.

Discourses Book 1, Chapter 18 is titled, 'That we ought not to be angry with the erring.' Here's the first few lines:

> If what the philosophers say is true, that in all people thought and action start from a single source, namely feeling–as in the case of assent the feeling that a thing is so, and in the case of dissent the feeling that it is not so, yes, and, by Zeus, in the case of suspended judgement the feeling that it is uncertain, so also in the case of impulse towards a thing, the feeling that it is expedient for me and that it is impossible to judge one thing expedient and yet desire another, and again, to judge one thing fitting, and yet to be impelled to another–if all this be true, why are we any longer angry with the multitude?–'They are thieves,' says someone, 'and robbers.'– What do you mean by 'thieves and robbers?' They have simply gone astray in questions of good and evil. Ought we, therefore, to be angry with them, or rather pity them?

Those opening lines concerning feeling, assent, dissent, judgement, and the like contain a quick rundown of Stoic psychology. So when Epictetus gets to "if all this be true, why are we any longer angry..." he's saying that accepting Stoicism's axioms concerning the human mind leaves no room for blame. We acknowledge that the offender could not have done any differently with the information and perspective that they had at the time. Instead of anger and offense, we are left with Stoic pity. It's an attitude that is free from anger and which is willing to engage with, and even assist the ignorant individual (through correction if possible, or simply through continued goodwill despite their offense). I suggest that it is essential that we apply that same Stoic pity towards our past selves.

You may be protesting that you can not pity your ignorance, because you knew better than to do what you did. And yes, in general, I suspect that all of us have the knowledge that rudeness, hatefulness, and bigotry are wrong. We understand that theft, and violence, and murder are bad. I have no doubt that most of us would accept these ideas. However, there is a difference between subscribing to a belief and embodying that belief. I used to shoplift as a young man. Not out of any need. Out of arrogance, for the sake of a thrill. I absolutely understood that theft was wrong. I was taught that, I could recite it, and I am certain that I would have protested if anything was taken from me. But in the end, I felt that taking something for myself was better than not doing so. My actions defined my true beliefs.

I'm not happy that I used to be that person, and it has been a very long time since I stole from another. Now I have a wider and deeper set of convictions, but I still dismiss them when it suits me. I've been bold enough to tell each of you to expect people to make mistakes and then let it go. But I still get angry at people from time to time. Why? Because I feel that acting on my anger will get me what I desire more quickly than acting Stoically would allow. I know better, but I don't believe better in that moment. In these moments I am displaying the same kind of ignorance that, hopefully, spurs me to be gracious to others. Those whose learning is complete blame neither themselves nor others. Can't we take pity on ourselves? Instead of lashing out with anger, or sulking in our disappointment, why not recognize that we are human and therefore fallible. Why not use our mistake as a lesson and instruct ourselves in better ways? Let's get back up when we fail, to celebrate behaving like a human –however imperfectly– and fully embrace the pursuit we've embarked on.

And finally, what exercise can get me back into my Stoic practice?
How do we rehabilitate our Stoicism? We write.

Writing was and is a Stoic philosophical exercise. Every line I read to you from Marcus Aurelius is part of a personal journal that he kept.

It was never meant to be published. Each chapter was a reminder to himself of the wisdom he had learned from others. He was recalling these lessons to combat his own failings. When Marcus wrote about the need to be gracious to the jerks he met in court, he had just finished dealing with a bunch of jerks in court. The Meditations are not filled with original thoughts. The Emperor was recalling Stoic teachings in order to apply them to his own unique situation. We should all be doing this. We should be examining our failures, uncovering better ways to act, and reminding ourselves of those better ways daily. Writing provides a means of conversing with yourself, for both admonishment and praise.

I began ImmoderateStoic.com in order to push myself to study and understand Stoicism. It is challenging to speak simply and clearly about a subject while still retaining the richness of the Stoic perspective. This constant practice of bringing old lessons back to mind and attempting to explain them has greatly enriched my life. Less publicly, I keep both a physical journal and a huge number of notes in the Evernote app. I keep the physical journal because the act of pen to paper writing commits thoughts to memory more readily than typing (that's just good science, look it up). I keep my Evernote journal because my phone is always with me, I can easily search through my notes, and I'd have to carry a library's worth of physical notebooks if I printed out all I had online.

Write about your philosophy. Recall your failures, find solutions, and commit both to paper. The next time you stumble you can look to see how you last recovered, and you can get over yourself that much quicker.

17

Physical Exercises

Good Fortune: Episode Ten

> The philosopher's body also must be well prepared for work because often virtues use it as a necessary tool for the activities of life…We will train both soul and body when we accustom ourselves to cold, heat, thirst, hunger, scarcity of food, hardness of bed, abstaining from pleasures, and enduring pains.

That line was from Musonius Rufus, once the head of the Stoic school. We might assume that an ancient philosophy school would of consist of a bunch of pampered rich kids endlessly attempting to show off their smarts by winning debates and making ridiculously pedantic points in general conversation. Frankly, I think that was often the case because Musonius and later Epictetus both are recorded giving lecture based smack downs to students who thought knowing about Stoicism was the same as living Stoicism. From Musonius in particular it becomes obvious that the true Stoic progressor necessarily make strong logical arguments, instead they take strong actions. They live a life of effort, an effort that concerns not just the mind but the whole self.

Hi, I'm Matt Van Natta and this is Good Fortune, in this episode we'll look into the physical practices of Stoicism. I'll be reading two different articles of mine, deep cuts from ImmoderateStoic.com. The first "Preparing for Life's Struggles," discusses the physicality of the Stoic school. Yes, philosophy concerns the life of the mind, but that mind is embodied, and we'll never flourish if we avoid aches and pains.

The second article is "Pain Don't Hurt," in which I quote Patrick Swazye from *Roadhouse* and talk about what I learned in a birthing class.

Alright, let's get physical…

Preparing for Life's Struggles

The ancient Stoics trained not just their minds, but also their bodies for the hard work of philosophy. The 'good flow of life' which they sought could not be grasped from books and lectures without additional toil. A simple lesson or a clever turn of phrase was never expected to overcome a lifetime of bad habits in the hearer. Stoic exercises, both mental and physical, were designed to take the lessons found on paper and write them into the life of the student. Because the universe will take things from us, the Stoics meditated on death and loss. Because life has lean times, they would eat plain foods or take no food at all. Stoics trained in order to be ready to meet the inevitable trials of life. We too must train if we want to be Stoic when it matters.

A clear expression of the physicality of the Stoic School can be found in the writings of Musonius Rufus. History leaves us very little of Musonius's words, but what we do have is illuminating. Unlike other Stoic texts, his give us insight into the daily practices at the Stoic school. For instance, he gives lessons on what foods Stoics should eat. He also gives job advice and lets loose some really horrible opinions concerning sexual relationships (always remember, we don't always have to pick up what ancient Greek guys are laying down). The ancient notes titled, By Musonius from the lecture on practicing philosophy, begin, "virtue…is not just theoretical knowledge, it is also practical, like both medical and musical knowledge. The doctor and the musician must each not only learn the principles of their own skill but be trained to act according to those principles. Likewise, the person who wants to be good must not only learn the lessons which pertain to virtue but train themself to follow them eagerly and rigorously." Stoicism is meant to be used in the field. What's the point in claiming indifference to the things we don't control if we continuously get angry at slow traffic? Stoicism is only Stoic when it is enacted, and that requires disciplined practice.

Therefore practicing each virtue always must follow learning the lessons appropriate to it, or it is pointless for us to learn about it.
(Musonius Rufus)

Stoic physical training was focused both on testing students' beliefs and building their mental endurance. Musonius Rufus did not care if his Stoics were under ten percent body-fat or how much they could deadlift. He was concerned that when they came face to face with pain they might choose comfort over virtue. The hard work of Stoicism involves desiring only what is good and avoiding only what is bad. Pain, according to Stoicism, is not actually a bad thing, it's simply indifferent. That's an easy enough idea to pay lip service to, but when pain stands between us and virtue, will we go through that pain or avoid it? Better to test ourselves in a controlled setting. Musonius said it this way, "the philosopher's body also must be well prepared for work because often virtues use it as a necessary tool for the activities of life…We will train both soul and body when we accustom ourselves to cold, heat, thirst, hunger, scarcity of food, hardness of bed, abstaining from pleasures, and enduring pains."

So what exercises did the ancients use to become better Stoics? We don't really know. History has taken that from us. The glimpses that we do have fall into the category of 'voluntary discomfort.' For instance, Epictetus advised that a thirsty person could wet their mouth, but then spit out the water. Seneca would eat bland but nutritious foods for long stretches. It would be interesting to see exactly how the ancient Stoics exercised, but there's no secret sauce, we simply need to train ourselves to follow Stoicism eagerly and rigorously. It isn't difficult to devise voluntary discomforts; hard beds, cold showers, and fasting come to mind. I happen to use an ice based practice that I learned in a birthing class. The point is not to make ourselves uncomfortable for discomfort's sake. We are meant to uncover the ingrained mental habits that go against Stoic thought, experience through disciplined exercise that those thoughts are wrong, and learn to consistently choose the wiser course.

Again, here are Musonius' thoughts on the matter,

> Indeed, those of us who have taken part in philosophical discussion obviously have heard and been exposed to the ideas that pain, death, poverty, and other things which are free of wickedness are in no way evil and, in turn, that wealth, life, pleasure or other things that have no share in virtue are not good. Nevertheless, even though we have heard these ideas, because of the corruption which has been ingrained in us all the way from childhood and because of the wicked behavior caused by this corruption, we think it a bad thing when pain comes on us, and we think it a good thing when pleasure comes. Likewise, we shudder at death as extreme misfortune, and we welcome life as the greatest good. When we give money away, we are distressed as if we are injured, and when we receive money, we rejoice as if we are helped. And in too many circumstances, we do not deal with our affairs in accordance with correct assumptions, but rather we follow thoughtless habit. Since I say that this is the case, the person who is practicing to become a philosopher must seek to overcome himself so that he won't welcome pleasure and avoid pain, so that he won't love living and fear death, and so that, in the case of money, he won't honor receiving over giving.

As modern Stoics, we seek to conquer the obstacles that come our way. We've turned to the words of an ancient school of thought and found, through practice, that Stoicism is replete with practical wisdom. It is the practice that proves the words. We are doing ourselves a disservice if we do not routinely exercise our philosophy. If we don't pack on some Stoic muscle, how will we be strong when real obstacles rise up before us? Be certain to not simply read the Stoics, participate along with them. Train yourself in the hard work of philosophy. The Stoic who pursues wisdom eagerly and rigorously is the one who obtains the good flow of life.

I believe in building up the will through physical effort. It's all well and good to hope that Stoicism can bring me through hard times, but I've seen my virtue derailed by a blood sugar crash due to skipping lunch! Am I going to choose the good when pain, physical or social, gets in the way? Stoic Week is coming up in November. I'll talk more about that later. Every year I like to choose a basic deprivation exercise to remind myself that whatever it is I'm giving up, I'm not actually deprived at all. This year I'm eating no food. Instead I'll be drinking the nutritional slurry known as Soylent. This week long abstinence from flavor should give my reason to meditate on my relationship to food. Do I spend too much effort chasing after novel experiences (I do like eating out) rather than simple, healthy food? Do I snack to cover up boredom or negative feelings? Who knows? Perhaps the break from routine will give me some answers.

In the following article, I talk about a practice I've adapted from a class about childbirth.

Pain Don't Hurt

> Pain don't hurt.
> (Patrick Swazye, *Road House*)

My wife and I are taking a birthing class in preparation for our daughter's arrival. The class presents a wide variety of methods to cope with stress and pain, so that both the pregnant woman and her partner can have as comfortable an experience as possible. In order to practice the breathing and mindfulness techniques against actual discomfort, participants take part in an exercise that I'm thinking of adding to my Stoic practice.

In the class, participants are asked to take ice, hold it in their hands, and find ways to work through the building pain. I find this method brilliant in its simplicity. For the price of a few melting ice cubes, I get a truly distracting experience to test myself against.

> When in pain remember that it brings no dishonor and that it does not weaken the governing intelligence. Pain is neither everlasting nor intolerable; it has its limits if you add nothing by imagination.
> (Marcus Aurelius)

In the class, the ice exercise is used with a variety of methods.

Sometimes we concentrate on our breath. Sometimes we pay attention to the sensation itself. Sometimes we visualize a scene in our minds. I say we, because that's what the teachers ask us to do. I actually have been using the time to practice applicable Stoic techniques, primarily Recitation and The Discipline of Assent.

Recitation on Ice

Holding ice in my hand, I reflect on Stoic quotes that apply to pain.
  For example,

> If you are distressed by anything external, the pain is not due to the thing itself, but to your estimate of it; and this you have the power to revoke at any moment.
>   (Marcus Aurelius)

I hold the ice for at least one minute, then I rest the hand. I continue with the opposite hand.

Assenting to Swazye-ism

Holding ice in my hand, I agree that pain does not, in fact, hurt.
  More seriously, I examine the impression that ice presents to my body. It is likely, as time goes on, that I will notice a judgement arising in my mind that pain is bad. Instead of assenting to this idea, I recognize that nothing outside of my volition is either good or bad, it is indifferent.
  I hold the ice for at least one minute, then I rest the hand. I continue with the opposite hand.

The Effect

I'm not looking to be a Spartan. In general, I feel we should pay attention to physical pain; it's there to let us know we need to respond to something. However, pain (neither physical nor emotional) should not distract us from our goal of a good flow of life. I've found that the addition of ice has a similar effect in my mental workouts that adding ankle weights when running would have on my physical ones. In our first birthing class session, I actual found the ice very painful. On the second session (with no practice in-between) I thought the teacher had halved the practice time. Nope, one minute each time. It went faster the second time because I regarded the sensations as indifferent.

Sometimes it's helpful to add potential discomfort to our routine in order to better practice our disciplines. Seneca said, "treat yourself harshly at times." Ice is a simple and effective way to do that. If you're looking for a means of putting your judgement to the test, I recommend filling an ice cube tray and getting to it.

18

Uprooting Fear

Good Fortune: Episode Eleven

There are more things likely to frighten us than there are to crush us; we suffer more in our imagination than in reality.

That's a line from Seneca's 13th letter to Lucilius. Titled, *On Groundless Fear*, this letter delves into all the mental miscalculations that make us humans slaves to fear. Another line from the letter reminds us that, "Some things torment us more than they should; some torment us before they should; and some torment us when they should not torment us at all. We are in the habit of exaggerating, or imagining, or anticipating, sorrow."

How can we stop doing this? How can we take control of our mind and make certain that fear can not take root there?

Today's questions:

- What's the Stoic view of fear and do Stoics experience it?
- The Stoics say that fear is all in my head but, if so, my head is really good at generating fear. What should I do about that?
- Outside of reigning in my imagination, how can I stoically confront fear?

Alright, let's get started…

What's the Stoic view of fear and do Stoics experience it?

Stoicism and emotions. Not exactly the peanut butter and chocolate of conversational topics. But before we can discuss fear, it's important to set up a scaffolding of Stoic concepts to support the conversation. So shake off all those cultural ideas of Stoics purging their emotions, eschewing joy, or any of that misguided stuff and settle in for a quick and probably inadequate primer on the Stoic approach to emotions.

The first thing we need to do is drop the term emotion. It's too loaded…with meaning. If you made a Venn diagram of the Stoic concepts we're going to be addressing and all those concepts contained in the word 'emotion' there would only be a sliver of overlap. The word I'm selecting to encompass the Stoic ideas of fear, anger, despair, etc…will be 'passion' or 'passions' as a plural. The expected benefit of using this somewhat archaic term is to arrest the listener. To cause us to stop and think about meaning, "why did he say passion instead of emotion?' Is there a difference?" Yes. There are many differences. For a much fuller understanding of those differences, I would direct you to a talk given by John Sellars during Stoic Week 2014, which I'll be certain to provide a link to on Immoderate Stoic. A quick quote from that talk, "the Stoics don't reject emotion, they reject passion, and that's quite a different thing."

In his talk, John Sellars lists four categories that fall within the concept of emotion. Three of those categories are fully embraced by Stoicism, meaning they are accepted as a necessary part of a fully human life. Only one aspect of human emotion is meant to be overcome and cast aside. That would be the passions.

Here are Sellar's categories in short:

First, emotions of affinity: Stoicism assumes that we are predisposed to care for ourselves, our close relatives, and, if we mature, we'll care for all humankind. In Stoicism it is not possible to flourish in life and remain emotionally indifferent to the well-being of others.

Next, emotions of shock: Even the mythical perfect Sage will experience goosebumps, blush, or be startled by a loud noise. Stoicism considers these to be natural physiological responses. We refer to them as pre-passions or, more poetically, "first movements of the soul."

There is nothing wrong with experiencing pre-passions, it's our reaction to those reactions that falls under Stoic scrutiny.

The third category is the one that Stoics seek to overcome. The Passions: A passion is an emotional response to an external state of affairs based on a mistaken value judgment. Passions stem from judgments, our judgments are of course, under our control (in Stoic psychology) and therefore here we can stand our ground. Here we can say, "I feel something, it's based on a mistaken belief, therefore I should change my belief which will change my feeling." It's not that our Stoic hearts are two sizes too small and therefore we turn our noses up at big bold feelings. It's that the passions are built on errors. Stoicism insists that if we allow ourselves to be driven by passions that are based on mistakes, we will live inconsistently and we will not thrive. The passion we'll be discussing, Fear, is defined as an irrational aversion or avoidance of an expected danger. Fear tosses away our present contentment simply because something might take it away later! Which is fundamentally ridiculous. Mistakes like that are what Stoicism admonishes us to avoid.

The fourth category, by the way, are Good Passions: positive emotional responses based on correct value judgments. Not only does Stoicism admit that good, lovely, worthy emotions are possible, the expectation is that a Stoic life will necessarily include those passions. A healthy mind includes a healthy emotional life.

So remember, part and parcel of a healthy human life are care and concern for others, natural physiological responses to the events of life, and positive passions based on proper value judgments.

So again: What's the Stoic view of fear and do Stoics experience it?

Passions are disorders of the soul. They are irrational responses to events. The direct products of faulty reasoning. Fear is an irrational aversion or avoidance of an expected danger. All fear, in the Stoic view, is groundless. So do Stoics experience it, of course! None of us are perfect. However, we do combat fear and *not* by simply suppressing it. Instead, we work to change the mistaken beliefs that generate and feed fear, so that it never takes root in the first place.

The Stoics say that fear is all in my head but, if so, my head is really good at generating fear. What should I do?

"Cease to harass your soul!" That's another Seneca quote. If we accept that fear is generated by our own judgments, then the emotional distress that we are combating is self-inflicted. We simply need to stop harassing ourselves.

Marcus Aurelius agreed with this line of reasoning and, thankfully, he wrote down advice concerning *how* to cease harassing our soul. We can find it in Book 7, Chapter 29 of his *Meditations*:

> Stop fantasizing! Cut the strings of desire that keep you dancing like a puppet. Draw a circle around the present moment. Recognize what is happening either to you or to someone else. Dissect everything into its causal and material elements. Ponder your final hour. Leave the wrong with the person who did it.

The Emperor doesn't want to waste his life working himself up over the unreal. To combat his wandering thoughts, he reminds himself of five stoic mental practices:

- Attend to the present moment
- Focus on what affects people here and now
- Break things down until they are understandable and manageable
- Remember that life is short
- Leave the wrong with the person who did it

The Stoic mind is rooted in the present. Seneca put it this way, "These two things must be cut away: fear of the future, and the memory of past sufferings. The latter no longer concern me, and the future does not concern me yet." If we focus on what we can do now, this minute, to make our lives better we can not only avoid ruminating on imagined future difficulties, we can know that we did our best to keep those difficulties from occurring. Aurelius reminds himself to open his eyes to the present environment, particularly concerning what is happening to himself and others.

I used to constantly worry about getting seated on time and and at the best possible table when going out to eat with friends. I can not tell you the number of pre-dinner conversations I failed to enjoy because I was busy worrying about whether the during-dinner conversations would happen on time. What a ridiculous but common way to approach life.

Aurelius also says to "break things down until they are understandable and manageable." So here we once again run into the Stoic practice of **physical definition**. A full explanation is found in Episode 3 of *Good Fortune* so I won't repeat myself here. Concerning fear, we can use physical definition to strip our imagined future down into parts and evaluate them from a Stoic perspective. In Letter 13 Seneca shares a series of questions developed for just that purpose.

"Put the question voluntarily to yourself: "Am I tormented without sufficient reason, am I morose, and do I convert what is not an evil into what is an evil?""

As was pointed out in the opening to this episode, we are in the habit of exaggerating, or imagining, or anticipating, sorrow.

Just a few days into Stoic Week 2015 I learned that I might not be able to purchase the house that I've spent the last month or so attempting to get. Some business about insurmountable permitting, zoning, blah blah blah issues. I've been a good Stoic during the entire home buying process so I haven't fully invested myself in the property and such, but still, when my loan guy called saying he thought the whole deal was dead, I got red in the face. Not anger or embarrassment, just a…I don't know, up-swelling of chemical "what the heck?!" A definite first movement of the soul. After that pre-passion I felt a few actual passions, no doubt. I was ok with losing the house, it wasn't even mine after all, but the idea of breaking the news to my wife and of going back into the house hunting process, now with significantly less time before our present lease was up…all of that was swimming in my head.

To ask myself Seneca's three questions: was I tormenting myself without reason? Well, nothing I felt was going to change my ability to purchase a house. Also, my family is in a good place in life. Not getting the house would be a setback but not deeply disruptive. Was I morose? Well, I hadn't had time to get into a funk concerning events, so no. And I can honestly report the same state today, by the way. Was I converting a non-evil into an evil? I was in danger of doing so. It did feel to me for a time that losing the house would be a bad thing. Which isn't true. After all, nothing about the house buying process has the ability to affect my virtue. I can thrive without any of it. So Stoically, I couldn't justify feeling fear, anger, or any other strong discontentment concerning the situation.

The process of stepping back and criticizing my initial judgments helped my find my footing. Continuing on and accepting my new judgments actually uprooted the passions that had begun to grow in my mind. And that is the Stoic goal. Never to suppress or ignore our fears, to uproot them completely through a radical change in perspective.

Outside of reigning in my imagination, how can I stoically confront fear?

When we really begin to face fear as a Stoic, we'll begin to relish the obstacle that it represents.

Listen to how Seneca lays it out at the end of Letter 13.

> But I am ashamed either to admonish you sternly or to try to beguile you with such mild remedies. Let another say. "Perhaps the worst will not happen." You yourself must say. "Well, what if it does happen? Let us see who wins! Perhaps it happens for my best interests; it may be that such a death will shed credit upon my life." Socrates was ennobled by the hemlock draught. Wrench from Cato's hand his sword, the vindicator of liberty, and you deprive him of the greatest share of his glory.

Seneca is saying that the fear avoidance tactic of hoping for the best, of wishful thinking, is weak sauce. The Stoic tactic isn't wishful thinking, it's unshakable thinking.

When he opens Letter 13 he commends his friend for already displaying a Stoic pride in battling life's ups and downs.

"I know that you have plenty of spirit; for even before you began to equip yourself with maxims which were wholesome and potent to overcome obstacles, you were taking pride in your contest with

Fortune; and this is all the more true, now that you have grappled with Fortune and tested your powers. For our powers can never inspire in us implicit faith in ourselves except when many difficulties have confronted us on this side and on that, and have occasionally even come to close quarters with us. It is only in this way that the true spirit can be tested, – the spirit that will never consent to come under the jurisdiction of things external to ourselves."

Strictly speaking, if we were perfect Stoics, we would never battle fear because we would never experience it. But we do experience fear, so we have to choose how to combat it. Our first option is to avoid the thing we fear. That leaves our emotional state in the hands of fate, which is unacceptable. We could also avoid thinking about our fears, assuage them by thinking cheerful thoughts like, "what are the chances the worst possible thing will happen?" The Stoic option is to attack fear at the root. We change the very judgments that create the fear. We change what we control, ourselves, our own mind, and make it better suited for the world as it is.

Now, it may seem that we are leaving a void where our passions used to be. Fear can, after all, drive us to actions. The passion of anger is often pointed to as supposed fuel for meaningful change. Well, we Stoics live according to nature and nature abhors a vacuum. The space where the passion of fear once was is meant to be filled by a 'good passion' in this case the Stoic concept named *Caution*.

Caution is the rational avoidance of an expected danger. Caution recognizes that there are things we can reasonably prefer to avoid as long as avoiding them doesn't lead to lack of virtue. In a previous episode I quoted Book 6 Chapter 20 of the *Meditations*, "In the ring, our opponents can gouge us with their nails or butt us with their heads and leave a bruise, but we don't denounce them for it or get upset with them or regard them from then on as violent types. We just keep an eye on them after that. Not out of hatred or suspicion, just keeping a friendly distance." That friendly distance is Caution; a simple, prudent step in keeping with wisdom. Notice that Caution doesn't cause us to get out of the ring. It's simply an adjustment of our stance as we happily continue to wrestle.

19

The Stoic Present

So Slender an Object

Don't panic before the picture of your entire life. Don't dwell on all the troubles you've faced or have yet to face, but instead ask yourself as each trouble comes, "What is so unbearable or unmanageable in this?" Your reply will embarrass you. Then remind yourself that it's not the future or the past that bears down on you, but only the present. Always the present, which becomes an even smaller thing when isolated in this way and when the mind that cannot bear up under so slender an object is chastened.
(*Meditations* 8:36)

The Stoic mindset is rooted in the present. The present is, after all, the only place where we can exercise mastery over what is in our control. The past is fixed and untouchable. The future is unknown. As one of my go-to Seneca quotes puts it, "These two things must be cut away: fear of the future, and the memory of past sufferings. The latter no longer concern me, and the future does not concern me yet." How much of our present stress is actually found in the present? Our worries come from an imagined future. Our shame comes from a past we can not change. If we put those intrusive thoughts aside and examine the present moment, what are we left with? I'd wager that 99% of the time, whatever distress remains is manageable.

I used to live under the burden of the future. For years I doubt an hour went by in which I didn't create some calamity in my head.

That toxic habit contributed to an anxiety/depression spiral that nearly killed me. It took additional years of practice to learn to stop damaging myself that way. Even now, I'm a very skilled doom predictor. Thankfully, I'm able to recognize and dismiss these fantasies as what the are, a piss poor use of the human mind.

Marcus Aurelius had similar issues. In Book 7, the emperor admonishes himself in quick succession with three statements:

- Wipe out the imagination
- Stop pulling the strings
- Confine yourself to the present

It seems Aurelius was more than capable of imagining his own bad endings. He probably had a lot of help from historical examples, being the Roman emperor and all. Aurelius kept reminding himself that panicking before the tyranny of the future was foolish, because nothing he foresaw was real. He needed to stop what-if-ing and pay attention to the present, where he could actually affect change.

Thoughts of the future are a subtle trap. It doesn't do us any good to pretend tomorrow isn't coming, after all*. But we don't just think, "I need to do x and y before tomorrow, and not forget to bring z." Instead, we create stories and invest emotionally in them. We live out fights at work that never come to pass. Our pulse races at imagined rejections. And worse yet, by pouring energy into these fantasies, our mind often writes that effort off as work actually done. We check the box on a confrontation with our spouse that never happened, only to rage all the more when the thing we never addressed happens again!

Live in the slender present. Drop the heavy stress of your imagination and do the lighter work that's here for you in the real world. It's freeing because, in the present, we find that we're capable people. And by doing the work of the present, we prepare ourselves for the actual future that will arrive. That's the best we get; the chance to fully participate in our own lives.

*Yes, we Stoics often take time to recognize that we could die at any instant, but it's still our duty to fulfill our tasks until the real end comes.

20

Stoics vs Obstacles and Uncertainty

> Why do you hesitate or second-guess yourself when you know perfectly well what ought to be done?
> (*Meditations* 10:12:1)

Stoics take action. This is evident both from Stoic teachings and from the lives of famous practitioners. Stoicism, well lived, frees us to tackle the hard problems of this world without regard for the obstacles that fortune throws our way. That said, how can we move forward rationally without full knowledge of what's ahead? Won't we make mistakes, waste our time, or even waste our very lives fighting unwinnable battles?

Emperor Aurelius asked himself these questions. His daily decisions shaped an empire. From time to time in his *Meditations*, we find Marcus Aurelius struggling against choice paralysis. Wouldn't it be best to make no moves until the perfect solution came along? It's understandable to want to know everything before making a decision, but that doesn't work for emperors and it won't work for us either. Thankfully, Marcus Aurelius gave himself a pep talk that laid out a Stoic approach to action.

> Why do you hesitate or second-guess yourself when you know perfectly well what ought to be done? If you know where you need to go, make a considerate but determined effort to get there. If you don't, wait and seek the best advice you can find. If you meet with resistance along the way, advance cautiously and prepare at any moment to

take refuge in what you know to be just, for to reach your goal justly is the apotheosis of achievement whereas to advance even one inch by doing an injustice is the most miserable form of failure. Relaxed but alert, cheerful but determined—such is reason's faithful follower.

(*Meditations* 10:12)

- If you know where to go, make a considerate but determined effort to get there.

The first point lays out the most obvious duty in Stoicism. If we know the right thing to do, then we do it. We don't ask what others will think or if they will stand in our way, such things are indifferent. We simply move towards the goal. Do we mow over the opposition to get our way? Of course not. Stoics treat people with respect, but we still do what is required.

- If you don't, wait and seek the best advice you can find.

The second point allows that sometimes we just don't know what the right move is. That's alright. It just means that the right thing to do is to learn the right thing to do. Stoics don't wander around aimless, we seek out directions.

- If you meet with resistance along the way, advance cautiously and prepare at any moment to take refuge in what you know to be just…

Obstacles may delay your efforts, but they can't touch your moral choices. Life throws us curve balls, but once again, we're expected to be indifferent to such things. Yes, unexpected resistance may challenge our projects. That's when we rely on our character.

- …for to reach your goal justly is the apotheosis of achievement whereas to advance even one inch by doing an injustice is the most miserable form of failure.

Stoicism does not support the idea that the ends justify the means. Stoics understand that how you reach your goal shapes the outcome.

Besides, we haven't invested our hope in whatever project is in front of us. Our goal is to be the best person we can be no matter the circumstances of life.

- Relaxed but alert, cheerful but determined–such is reason's faithful follower.

Aurelius's final point is a mental posture: *relaxed but alert, cheerful but determined*. It sounds like he's repeating something, doesn't it? I hear this line as something Stoics said under their breath as they faced the trials of the day. Relaxed but alert, cheerful but determined–such is reason's faithful follower. This is how Stoics are meant to be; cheerfully engaged with the real world as we seek to build a better one.

Stoics expect obstacles and uncertainty. Such things can't dissuade us from our goals. If we know what is right, if we know where we need to go, there is no room for second-guessing. So let's go out there ready to meet resistance with grit and good cheer.

21

Frightened of Change

Good Fortune: Episode Twelve

Frightened of change? But what can exist without it? *What's closer to nature's heart?* Can you take a hot bath and leave the firewood as it was? Eat food without transforming it? Can any vital process take place without something being changed? Can't you see? It's just the same with you – and just as vital to nature.
(*Meditations* 7:18)

There's lots of talk about the unshakable mountain that is, "The Stoic." Yet change is closest to nature's heart, according both to Aurelius' line and to Stoic philosophy. And the Stoic, of course, follows nature. So how does one find solid ground in an ever-changing universe?

Hi, I'm Matt Van Natta and this is Good Fortune. I'm glad to be back. Since podcasts don't have to be listened to the day they're available, let me explain that this is the first episode after almost five month long break and also the first episode of 2016. I am grateful for the many requests to get this podcast going again. It's gratifying to know your listening.

Spring is upon us so I thought it only natural to start by talking about death. Ha-ha. I think it's time. We Stoics are famous for a fixation on mortality and, in my opinion, avoiding our philosophy's teachings concerning death denies us a rich vein of practical wisdom. In fact, I've been unable to address a variety of requested topics because, to cover the various losses in life (relationships, jobs, dignity, etc...) I need to be able to point back towards the Stoic approach to the loss OF life. So Death is coming, in Episode 13. First we lay the groundwork. Because before we can wrestle with that great, final change, we have to understand that in the Stoic universe, change is accepted as a constant.

Today's questions:

- Exactly how close to nature's heart is change?
- So the ancient Stoics were really hung up on change, what's it matter?
- What are the benefits of perceiving and accepting that the universe is ever-changing?

Alright, let's get started...

Exactly how close to nature's heart is change?

In Book 7 of *Meditations*, Aurelius reminds himself multiple times of the nature of the universe. In Chapter 23 he says, "Nature takes substance and makes a horse. Like a sculptor with wax. And then melts it down and uses the material for a tree. Then for a person. Then for something else. Each existing only briefly. It does the container no harm to be put together, and none to be taken apart." Just two thoughts latter, in Chapter 25, he notes that, "Before long, nature, which controls it all, will alter everything you see and use it as material for something else – over and over again. So that the world is continually renewed."

I can't say why the Emperor was so fixated on transformation during this time, but in Book 7, Chapter 18, (the quote I opened with) he asks himself if he is frightened of change. It's a serious question for a Stoic. The school's founder, Zeno, asked us to "live according to nature." For a pious Stoic like Aurelius, nature was not only the right path, but his god, Zeus. And the god of the universe, the god that *was* the universe, was the one described by Heraclitus.

Have you heard that you can never step twice into the same stream? That was Heraclitus, as quoted by Plato. Heraclitus played a profound role in describing the Stoic universe. He claimed that, "everything changes and nothing stands still," also translated, "everything flows

Frightened of Change   103

and nothing remains." The Stoics adopted Heralitus' flux and his ever flowing universe is at the core of the Stoic perception of the world.

For instance, listen to *Meditations* Book 10, Chapter 7, where Aurelius ponders a variety of possible universes,

> The whole is compounded by nature of individual parts, whose destruction is inevitable ("destruction" here means transformation). If the process is harmful to the parts and unavoidable, then it's hard to see how the whole can run smoothly, with parts of it passing from one state to another, all of them built only to be destroyed in different ways. Does nature set out to cause its components harm, and make them vulnerable to it – indeed, predestined to it? Or is it oblivious to what goes on? Neither one seems very plausible.
> But suppose we throw out "nature" and explain these things through inherent properties. It would still be absurd to say that the individual things in the world are inherently prone to change, and at the same time be astonished at it or complain – on the grounds that it was happening "contrary to nature." And least of all when things return to the state from which they came. Because our elements are simply dispersed, or are subject to a kind of gravitation – the solid portions being pulled toward earth, and what is ethereal drawn into the air, until they're absorbed into the universal logos – which is subject to periodic conflagrations, or renewed through continual change.
> And don't imagine either that those elements – the solid and the ethereal – are with us from our birth. Their influx took place yesterday, or the day before – from the food we ate, the air we breathed.
> And that's what changes – not the person your mother gave birth to…

Here Marcus pits his favored view of the universe, as providential and purposeful, against a universe of unthinking atoms. It's a fascinating discussion, but what I want to point out is that the fundamental nature of both worldviews is change. Providence and atoms are contested, but the flow is not. For the Stoic, change is a given. And as such, it becomes unreasonable to complain about change as if it were unexpected. As the Emperor says elsewhere, "How ridiculous and how strange to be surprised at anything which happens in life."

I also want to focus in on those final thoughts of Book 10 Chapter 7. "And don't imagine either that those elements – the solid and the ethereal – are with us from our birth. Their influx took place yesterday, or the day before – from the food we ate, the air we breathed. And that's what changes – not the person your mother gave birth to." Stoic change goes further than the eventual death of a horse, or felling of a tree. We are transformed daily. The child my mother gave birth to nearly forty years ago has already left the world, even though I happen to be here. Yes, Stoics are expecting and accepting the great changes of life, but our perception is supposed to go further; towards a realization that nothing is ever still. A certain stretch of river may be slow, but it's ever and always flowing.

So the ancient Stoics were really hung up on change, what's it matter?

If we never come to terms with change, we'll never gain the benefits that Stoicism can provide. Chapter 2 of the *Enchiridion* begins, "Remember that the promise of desire is the attainment of what you desire, that of aversion is not to fall into what is avoided, and that he who fails in his desire is unfortunate, while he who falls into what he would avoid experiences misfortune. If then, you avoid only what is unnatural among those things which are under your control, you will fall into none of the things which you avoid; but if you try to avoid disease, or death, or poverty, you will experience misfortune."

A similar sentiment is found in Chapter 31 of the *Enchiridion*, where Epictetus speaks of piety towards the gods. Piety is a term you won't find me addressing very often. First, because I try to develop Good Fortune in a way that speaks to as diverse a group of listeners as possible. Second, because my personal approach to Stoicism is non-theistic in nature. However, Epictetus, Aurelius, Musonius Rufus, these were pious men; true followers of Zeus as they understood him. Their god was quite different than the sort of god I was raised with, and even different than many of their contemporaries might have accepted.

As the ancient historian Diogenes Laertius put it, "They also say that God is an animal, immortal, rational, perfect in happiness, immune to all evil, providentially taking care of the world and of all that is in the world, but he is not of human shape. He is the creator of the universe, and as it were, the Father of all things in common, and that a part of him pervades everything, which is called by different names, according to its powers..." This Zeus, this animal that is the whole universe, is ever changing, growing, expressing new things. To live wisely, rationally, is to understand his self-expression and to accept it no matter what.

> In piety toward the gods, I would have you know, the chief element is this, to have right opinions about them – as existing and as administering the universe well and justly – and to have set yourself to obey them and submit to everything that happens, and to follow it voluntarily, in the belief that it is being fulfilled by the highest intelligence. For if you act in this way, you will never blame the gods, nor find fault with them for neglecting you. **But this result cannot be secured in any other way than by withdrawing your idea of the good and evil from the things which are not under our control, and in placing it in those which are under our control, and in those alone.** Because, if you think any of those former things to be good or evil, then, when you fail to get what you want and fall into what you do not want, it is altogether inevitable that you will blame and hate those who are responsible for the results. For this is the nature of every living creature, to flee from and turn aside from the things that appear harmful, and all that produces them. Therefore, it is impossible for a man who thinks he is being hurt to take pleasure in that which he thinks is hurting him, just as it is impossible to take pleasure in the hurt itself. Hence it follows that even a father is reviled by a son when he does not give his child some share in the things that seem to be good...That is why the farmer reviles the merchant, and those who have lost their wives and their

children. For where a man's interest lies, there is also his piety…
(*Enchiridion* 31)

Epictetus' claim is that the universe is guided by a great intelligence therefore to be angry at the unfolding of that universe is to be angry at the gods. My opinion is closer to Marcus Aurelius' second possible world from Book 10, Chapter 7, that if I accept that the universe is bound by its own laws to play out as it does, then it is irrational to be angry at the outcome. I can scold myself for stubbing my toe, but yelling at the chair is foolish.

Epictetus says that in order to gain anything from Stoicism we have to withdraw our conception of good and evil from the ever-changing world and root it in ourselves. The good is found in interacting wisely with the world as it is, the evil; in reacting poorly to that same world. Why does acceptance of change matter? Anything less cuts us off from Stoic serenity and joy.

What are the benefits of perceiving and accepting that the universe is ever-changing?

The wise will start each day with thought; Fortune gives us nothing which we can really own.

Nothing, whether public or private, is stable; the destinies of men, no less than those of cities, are in a whirl.

Whatever structure has been reared by a long sequence of years, at the cost of great toil and through the great kindness of the gods, is scattered and dispersed in a single day. No, he who has said 'a day' has granted too long a postponement to swift misfortune; an hour, an instant of time, suffices for the overthrow of empires.

How often have cities in Asia, how often in Achaia, been laid low by a single shock of earthquake? How many towns in Syria, how many in Macedonia, have been swallowed up? How often has this kind of devastation laid Cyprus in ruins?

We live in the middle of things which have all been destined to die.

Mortal have you been born, to mortals have you given birth.

Reckon on everything, expect everything.

You may recognize Seneca's premeditation. I've mentioned it before. So Seneca backs up Aurelius and Epictetus. The wise will start each day dwelling on change. Why? To become fatalistic? Life will happen as life happens so accept it and carry on? NO. We acknowledge the instability of the world so that we remember to put our energy into building up what can be stable, the only thing that can be, ourselves.

I'm recording this episode while surrounded by favorite books, art pieces, and whiskey decanters. I'm very fortunate to be able to create a space that is particularly well suited to me. I'm amazingly fortunate to have a wife who encouraged me to do so! I can breath easy in this study. What if a thief breaks in tomorrow? What if a fire turns it all to ash? Would I still breath easy? Way back in episode two I shared a quote from Keith Seddon that I will repeat again, "We must invest our hopes not in the things that happen, but in our capacities to face them as human beings." I return to that quote regularly because it illuminates the heart of the Stoic worldview. The Stoic seeks to be virtuous no matter the circumstances of life. Just, always. Wise, always. Tempered, always. Courageous, always. The fruit of that virtue, serenity, is equally constant. In fact, Epictetus claims that, "no feature of serenity is so characteristic as continuity and freedom from hindrance." If we don't realize and internalize that the thing we're enjoying is impermanent by the very fact that it exists, then we will be disturbed the second it changes. I'm not trying to shame us because we aren't perfect unperturbed Sages. But if we seek our peace in the present environment instead of in spite of it, we're not even walking the Stoic path.

The benefit of orienting ourselves to the flux of the world is that we can learn to love it as it is. We can stop waiting for happiness in some imagined perfect future and start really living in this moment. How? Well, the ancient Stoics advised continuously wrestling with that most striking of changes, Death. But that's next episode.

22

Death and an Epitaph For Ourselves

Good Fortune: Episode Thirteen

> Keep before your eyes day by day death and exile, and everything that seems terrible, but most of all death; and then you will never have any abject thought, nor will you yearn for anything beyond measure.
> (*Enchiridion* 21)

How do you react to those words? Are they sobering? Off putting? Depressing? I could understand any of those responses and more.

Hi, I'm Matt Van Natta and this is Good Fortune. Today we'll be addressing the Stoic view of death and the Stoic insistence that confronting the fact of death is a useful exercise. Death is a huge topic and this podcast tends to come in at around 15 minutes, so please understand that we'll be covering only a glint of a facet of what the philosophy has to say. Also, this episode rests on the foundation of Episode 12, titled "Frightened of Change?" I'd suggest listening to it first.

Today's questions:

- What is death, to the Stoic?
- Why should we continuously confront death?
- How can we come to accept death?

Alright, let's get started...

What is death, to the Stoic?

You may remember Book 7, Chapter 23 of *Meditations* from episode twelve, "Nature takes substance and makes a horse. Like a sculptor with wax. And then melts it down and uses the material for a tree. Then for a person. Then for something else. Each existing only briefly. It does the container no harm to be put together, and none to be taken apart." To the Stoics, death is harmless. The universe, of which we are a part, is in a constant state of change; death is but a word for one of processes that bring about that change. Simple, right?

Of course not. Death shakes the pillars of the earth. The death of a loved one can not only debilitate us through grief but force a complete restructuring of our lives. The ancient Stoics were aware of the impact of death, they lived as closely with it as anyone else. And still, Stoic quotes abound with shrugs towards mortality. It isn't difficult to find seemingly flippant or cold comments; comparing dead loved ones to broken clay pots, for instance. So what gives? Is death completely meaningless to Stoics? No. Death is real. It's a fact. As such, death has to be addressed. However, people can build their entire lives (entire societies) around avoiding the fact of mortality. Both the Greek and Roman Stoics lived in such times. They were willing to question those societal norms. The Stoics asked, "what is a healthy response to death?" With death as a certainty, what is to be done?

The Stoics wanted to shape their understanding of death in a way that accorded with reality. Part of that relearning relied on thoughts like Emperor Aurelius' horse-to-tree-to-human quote. Death *is*, and death is unavoidable. The other half of their relearning had to do with meaning we attach to death.

In the *Enchiridion*, Chapter 5, Epictetus is recorded as saying, "It is not the things themselves that disturb people, but their judgments about those things. For example, death is nothing dreadful, or else Socrates too would have thought so, but the judgment that death is dreadful, this is the dreadful thing…" To pick up Epic's point, people understandably wail at the loss of their loved ones, but they sometimes rejoice at the death of their enemy. They grieve the the loss of a child much differently then the death of their elders, particularly if the final years were painful ("it's a blessing, really"). The Stoic insistence is that we shape our reactions to death, the Stoic challenge is to reshape our judgments in a way that not only accepts, but embraces the fact that everything is mortal.

Why should we continuously confront death?

"Furthermore, at the very moment when you are taking delight in something, call to mind the opposite impressions. What harm is there if you whisper to yourself, at the very moment you are kissing your child, and say, 'Tomorrow you will die'? So likewise to your friend, 'Tomorrow you will go abroad, or I shall, and we shall never see each other again'? –Nay, but these are words of ill omen. –Yes, and so are certain incantations, but because they do good, I do not care about that, only let the incantation do us good. But do you call anything ill-omened except those which signify some evil for us? Cowardice is ill-omened, a mean spirit, grief, sorrow, shamelessness; these are words of ill-omen. And yet we ought not to hesitate to utter even these words, in order to guard against the things themselves." (*Discourses* 3:24:85-90)

That first advice is harsh, yes? I found it mildly shocking when I first read the Enchiridion, decades before becoming a father. Now, as a father, it's...challenging. Why would a Stoic teacher advise such a potentially off-putting practice? Over the years, wrestling with and returning to the many Stoic admonitions to dwell on death, I've concluded that the hope and expectation of the ancient teachers was that their students, that we, would find the practice freeing.

The act of confronting death provides a scalpel with which we can cut away the extraneous aspects of our life. It can allow us to be our best self now. To fully love now, be attentive now, enact justice now. "Keep before your eyes day by day...death; and then you will never have any abject thought, nor will you yearn for anything beyond measure." What better way to instill an urgency to be better than to remember every morning that we are not promised tomorrow?

I love every moment with my daughter. Still, I've tossed away plenty of experiences with her while staring at a screen, whether it's a TV, laptop, or phone. I've lost out on time with friends by either passing on time together out of laziness or not giving them my attention when

I am technically present. Same for my wife. Outside of these close relationships I've also not invested fully in my community for similar reasons. What a waste. I don't have eternity.

What harm is there if I think to myself when kissing my daughter, "tomorrow you will die, Freyja?" I have done this. I've meditated on it. It's quite the splash of cold water to the face. In my own life, the practice snaps my attention right back to my girl. I put the phone down. I listen to and answer her questions. I relate. And in living fully in that relationship, I not only appreciate what I have, but invest in making it even better.

I don't dwell on how any of my loved ones could pass. The practice isn't meant to be some CSI-style voyeurism. I work to internalize a fact. Mortal I was born, to me mortals have been born. I can't spent every minute soaking in the joy of parenthood. There's other stuff to do. But when I choose those other things, which ones make sense?

The Stoic focus on death is not simply meant as "You Only Live Once," advice. But that is part of it, and it's worth taking seriously.

How can we come to accept death?

If you, like myself, have been raised to deny mortality, to shun death, and to never speak of the raw fact that we all will die then we have much to unlearn. We have to struggle to uncouple ourselves from the fear of inevitable change. It requires practice, daily practice, or we will never gain an honest perception of the world.

There are plenty of materials available for the standard Stoic death meditations and practices. I'll link to them on ImmoderateStoic.com. I would like, instead, to look at a simple practice found in Marcus Aurelius' Meditations. Here is Book 10, Chapter 8 in full:

> Epithets for yourself: Upright. Modest. Straightforward. Sane. Cooperative. Disinterested.
> Try not to exchange them for others.
> And if you should forfeit them, set about getting them back.
> Keep in mind that 'sanity' means understanding things –

each individual thing – for what they are. And not losing the thread.

And 'cooperation' means accepting what nature assigns you – accepting it willingly.

And 'disinterest' means that the intelligence should rise above the movements of the flesh – the rough and the smooth alike. Should rise above fame, above death, and everything like them.

If you maintain your claim to these epithets – without caring if others apply them to you or not – you'll become a new person, living a new life. To keep on being the person that you've been – to keep being mauled and degraded by the life you're living – is to be devoid of sense and much too fond of life. Like those animal fighters at the games – torn half to pieces, covered in blood and gore, and still pleading to be held over until tomorrow…to be bitten and clawed again.

Set sail, then, with this handful of epithets to guide you. And steer a steady course if you can. Like an emigrant to the islands of the blessed. And if you feel yourself adrift – as if you've lost control – then hope for the best, and put in somewhere where you can regain it. Or leave life altogether, not in anger, but matter-of-factly, straightforwardly, without arrogance, in the knowledge that you've at least done that much with your life.

And as you try to keep these epithets in mind, it will help you a great deal to keep the gods in mind as well. What they want is not flattery, but for rational things to be like them. For figs to do what figs were meant to do – and dogs, and bees…and people.

Here the Emperor has chosen simple adjectives to describe his character. Where does he visualize these words? On his tomb. The Stoic Seneca once said, "if one does not know to which port one is sailing, no wind is favorable." Aurelius is setting his destination. A moral destination.

One of my favorite epitaphs can be found in the movie *The Royal*

Tenenbaums. In it, the self-centered title character has these words carved on his headstone, "Died tragically rescuing his family from the wreckage of a destroyed sinking battleship." He did not die that way. He simply saw the same words on a different man's tomb and decided to plagiarize that life after death.

Aurelius' Stoic epithet isn't about specific actions or projects at all (real or aspirational). When choosing his destination, he doesn't aim at things he can't control. Expanding the empire further. Turning the citizens and slaves of Rome into Stoics. Outliving his children. He sets a moral destination. Upright. Modest. Cooperative. This is a destination he can reach if he so chooses. This is a destination that can't be taken from him even if the empire is wrested from his hand. On his last day, whenever and wherever that would be, he hoped that the course of his life would lead observers to chisel those words in granite. We can do this as well. We can describe the character we want and aim for it. We can work to live up to our death.

I would challenge us to write our own epithets. To pick a few words that describe our ideal character and meditate on them with mortality on the mind. What must I do in *this* moment to be *that* person. What projects should I begin to aim at the life Stoicism offers? What projects should I end?

We are mortal. Our past is already gone. Our future isn't promised. This moment is what we have to work with. As Aurelius admonished, stop arguing about what a good person is and be one.

23

On Stoic Authority

You Shouldn't Eat That

I've recently found more than a few Stoics arguing against new ideas by saying, "that's not what Epictetus/Aurelius/Seneca said...so there." I assume these Stoics are all vegetarians.

> [Musonius Rufus] often talked in a very forceful manner about food, on the grounds that food was not an insignificant topic and that what one eats has significant consequences. In particular, he thought that mastering one's appetites for food and drink was the beginning of and basis for self-control.
>
> (Musonius Rufus, *Lectures and Sayings*)

The great Stoic teacher Musonius Rufus, claims that we should be lacto-vegetarians. In fact, he wants us all to be raw food vegetarians! Musonius had a variety of reasons to back up his claims. Our food choices are directly relate to our self-control. Our nature demands nutrition, but does not require pleasure. Also, meat makes people dim-witted. So, since Musonius was not only a headmaster of the ancient Stoic school but none other than the teacher of Epictetus, obviously all modern Stoics must become raw food lacto-vegetarians.

Nope. We don't have to adopt that practice. Modern Stoics can, and should, look into the reasoning Musonius Rufus lays out concerning food choices, but we can come to our own conclusions concerning what is appropriate to eat. And why can we do this? Is it because the subject of food is outside the scope of meaningful Stoic practice? No. Not in the least. Musonius is not just laying out ancient Roman nutritional advice. He is adamant that how we eat is a matter of virtue. It is not incidental. How we eat is just as important to wrestle with as whether or not we accept the Stoic concept of divinity, or the Stoic conception of the mind. The reason modern Stoics can disregard Musonius' point of view (or accept it) is because we are equal in authority to him, if we are equal to the task of thinking as a Stoic.

> I do not bind myself to some particular one of the Stoic masters. I too have a right to form an opinion.
> (Seneca)

Stoicism has not come to us from anything greater than the human mind. The ancient writings we have available consist of some class notes, letters to friends, a journal, and explanations that were written down by rival schools in order to refute them. None of our forethinkers were holy men and what they wrote wasn't gospel. Some had original minds and others were simply repeating what they were taught, but all of them were regular people who happened to subscribe to a similar point of view. At times, "similar" might be considered a stretch.

Epictetus does not seem to be as adamant as his teacher was, concerning the subject of food. There's no record of him denying people the enjoyment of a perfectly cooked steak. Not to say he didn't believe in a proper diet. Chapter 46 of the *Enchiridion* mentions that we should not, "…talk about how persons ought to eat, but eat as you ought." So there is a right way to eat. For Epictetus, the Stoic diet was one of self-control and social grace.

> …at a feast, to choose the largest share is very suitable to the bodily appetite, but utterly inconsistent with the social spirit of an entertainment.
> (*Enchiridion* 36)

Epictetus taught his students to be disciplined concerning food. The scene he usually set was a banquet where all the delicacies of Roman society would be available to choose from. Epictetus didn't ask that we avoid meat, he wanted us to avoid gluttony. He wanted us to take into account the social nature of a party, and understand that the food is there to share, not to gorge upon. This approach to food was similar to the approach to life that Epictetus advocated; act with discipline and take the good of others into account. Once you look past the specifics of Musonius's dietary advice, you find a similar message at the core of his teachings, "...since these and other mistakes are connected with food, the person who wishes to be self-controlled must free himself of all of them and be subject to none. One way to become accustomed to this is to practice choosing food not for pleasure but for nourishment, not to please his palate but to strengthen his body." He saw food as a daily means of testing our willpower. Will we eat wisely, or will we eat Twinkies?

My point is not to dwell on food, though I find the subject interesting. My point is that Stoics can, and do, hold different opinions. Even two Stoics as well respected as Musonius Rufus and Epictetus held divergent opinions and emphasized different aspects of the philosophy. These men were contemporaries and the entire philosophical school was handed from one to the other, yet their teachings still varied. We should expect that modern Stoics will approach the philosophy in a way that the ancients did not anticipate. In fact, with the quantity and quality of information we moderns have, we should be improving Stoicism instead of resting on the snippets of past thoughts that happened to make it to the present day. Of course, Stoicism can't incorporate just any belief whatsoever. If someone claimed that emotions are the best and sole guide to good living they couldn't claim that Stoicism backs them up. There are core ideas in our philosophy that truly matter. You can see that as Musonius and Epictetus approach food. One man is really specific about the Stoic diet, the other seems to have a wider view, but both are concerned with moral virtue and mental and physical well-being.

Quoting ancient philosophers is a great way to point out a long-standing argument, or emphasize a Stoic point of view, but the words of these men don't end our discussions. It frankly isn't Stoic to appeal to authority. The ancients are dead. We are here and alive. Stoicism, if it has any value, is a living philosophy. We are its philosophers. We have the right to an opinion. Stoicism has held up pretty well since 300 BCE and we aren't going to break it with our poking and prodding. But we do know more about humanity and the universe than the ancient Greeks and Romans. We have the responsibility to incorporate that knowledge into the philosophy. For those of us who take up Stoicism as our way of life, the canon isn't closed. Do not accept what the ancients said without argument. Instead, improve their arguments. Build a more effective Stoicism. We are proof that Stoicism isn't done yet, so don't let others act like its last useful thought was written down in a scroll.

24

A Wish for Your Good Fortune

> Misfortune born nobly is good fortune.
> (Marcus Aurelius)

The title of my podcast and of this handbook comes from a simple line by Emperor Aurelius. To the Stoic, every moment is an opportunity to have good fortune, because every moment is an opportunity to be our best self. We seek to orient our lives according to the virtues of Justice, Wisdom, Temperance, and Courage while acknowledging that everything but our own opinions and actions are outside of our direct control. Practicing this mindset is easier said than done. As I write and record myself, I get the opportunity to present my best thoughts and edit those ideas into something that sounds authoritative. It's quite a privilege; one that I do not get to have in my day to day life. My lived experience is a messy one, at best. I stumble. I pick myself up. I abandon my principles and then take them up again all in a single hour. I hope, and sometimes believe, that the trajectory of my Stoicism has been moving towards consistency. However, when it comes to a need for improvement, there is no end in sight.

Every day we experience misfortunes. Life is filled with obstacles. Not every project we begin will find its way to completion. And yet, every moment we experience contains an opportunity to live well. We can always be victorious, we can forever have good fortune, if we decide that our primary aim is to do our best. And so, always remember, "misfortune born nobly is good fortune," and therefore I wish you good fortune always.

Good Fortune Episodes

Episode One
Untitled: April 2nd, 2015
Episode Two
A Stoic Start to the Day: April 16th, 2015
Episode Three
Attention is Fundamental: May 7th, 2015
Episode Four
What We Control: May 21st, 2015
Episode Five
A Stoic End to the Day: June 4th, 2015
Episode Six
Handling Distressing News: July 3rd, 2015
Episode Seven
When People Are Obstacles, July 16th, 2015
Episode Eight
When We Stumble: August 6th, 2015
Episode Nine
Resources: September 4th, 2015
Episode Ten
Physical Exercises: September 17th, 2015
Episode Eleven
Uprooting Fear: November 15th, 2015
Episode Twelve
Frightened of Change?: March 18th, 2016
Episode Thirteen
Death and an Epitaph for Ourselves: September 27th, 2016

Questions Asked and Answered

- Why title it Good Fortune? 3
- What's with the Raven? 3
- I want a boisterous crowd to shut up and go away, how can Stoicism help? 5
- Are you a morning person? 9
- Have you prepared for the annoyances of the day? 10
- Are there any Stoic practices that can help me start the day right? 13
- How hard is it to think like a Stoic? 24
- How do we develop a consistent Stoic orientation towards the world? 25
- What sort of practice can help us keep a Stoic orientation towards life? 25
- How can I become invincible? 29
- How can we internalize what is under our control? 31
- If Stoic invincibility is achievable, what would that life look like? 33
- Is there a Stoic way to go to sleep? 17
- Is it possible to do Stoic exercises incorrectly? 19
- How are Stoics supposed to react to news, particularly the bad kind? 36
- Stoics use the term 'indifferent' a lot, what do you mean by that? 38
- Is there anything I can do to feel more in control after receiving bad news? 39
- What do I do when people are life's obstacles? 43
- How can I remain my best self when everyone else is being their worst self? 45
- When does a Stoic call it quits? 47
- How am I supposed to react when I screw up? 73
- How can I stop blaming myself (should I stop blaming myself) when the fact is I really did do something wrong? 75
- What exercise can get me back into my Stoic practice? 77
- What's the Stoic view of fear and do Stoics experience it? 88
- What should I do about fear? 90

- How can I Stoically confront fear? 92
- Exactly how close to nature's heart is change? 102
- The ancient Stoics were hung up on change, what does that matter? 104
- What are the benefits of perceiving and accepting that the universe is ever-changing? 106
- What is death, to the Stoic? 110
- Why should we continuously confront death? 111
- How can we come to accept death? 112

Recommended Resources

Modern

How to Be a Stoic by Massimo Pigliucci
Stoicism and the Art of Happiness by Donald Robertson

Ancient

Meditations by Marcus Aurelius
The Enchiridion of Epictetus

A more extensive list can be found at ImmoderateStoic.com. These four books are listed as a starting point for any person embarking on a modern Stoic journey.

Made in the USA
Middletown, DE
18 December 2019